a woman's huts
and hideaways

a woman's huts and hideaways

more than 40 she sheds and other retreats

Gill Heriz

with photography by
Nicolette Hallett

CICO BOOKS
LONDON NEW YORK

For Beatrix and Penny

Published in 2016 by CICO Books
An imprint of Ryland Peters & Small Ltd
20–21 Jockey's Fields   341 E 116th St
London WC1R 4BW   New York, NY 10029

www.rylandpeters.com

10 9 8 7 6 5 4 3 2

Text © Gill Heriz 2016
Design and photography © CICO Books 2016

A CIP catalog record for this book is available from
the Library of Congress and the British Library.

ISBN: 978 1 78249 322 8

Printed in China

Editor: Gillian Haslam
Designer: Alison Fenton
Photographer: Nicolette Hallett

In-house editor: Miriam Catley
Art director: Sally Powell
Production manager: Gordona Simakovic
Publishing manager: Penny Craig
Publisher: Cindy Richards

Contents

This book looks at more than forty amazing cabins, huts, hideaways, studios, and tiny homes, created by women as their own personal spaces. Some are in hidden places and others are on view, some are solitary spaces and others are designed for social gatherings, but most have some sense of retreat—a place to get work done, to meditate, to think, to create.

As the concept of women's sheds has become more popular, women are found pacing the spaces at the bottom of their gardens, inspired by the wonderful examples that can be seen in books, on social media, and in the press. Women tell me, again and again, "I want a shed, too" and, even better, "I am getting a shed!" It seems that women love the sense of being hidden and private from the world.

This collection of huts and hideaways follows on from my previous book, *A Woman's Shed*, and explores other types of retreats. In the heart of busy cities, by the water, and in the countryside, behind urban houses, up hills, and in the woods, we found a beautiful range of small-scale buildings, from a bus to an ice-cream van, an Airstream caravan to a tree-house, cob and mud huts, and tiny houses built on trailer bases.

I asked women how their hideaway came about, what they did in these personal spaces, and how they feel about having this place of their own. I felt so privileged to hear their extraordinary stories and their journeys—some hard and complex—and their inspirations. I heard about the communities, families, and friends who helped the women acquire, convert, or build. There is creativity and courage, humor and hard work, and sheer determination.

We found a huge and wonderful variety of buildings and met great women who welcomed us into gardens and backyards, fields and woods. The huts and hideaways come in a range of sizes and materials, and are put to varying uses. Some are converted outbuildings or garages, some are new constructions that have been built for purpose, some are built to take advantage of the beauty of their surroundings and the views, some are inherited and made anew with

wonderful interiors. One humble shed has been turned into a homage to a woman's life, while another shed multitasks as a studio, a wildlife lookout, a meditation space, and somewhere to keep garden tools.

Tiny homes are solutions to modern living, with the choice to live this way made for economic, personal, and aesthetic reasons. This is a relatively new phenomenon (we came across it when visiting Portland, Oregon, where we photographed several homes built on trailer bases) for young people who will never afford houses—or don't want them—and, for others, this offers the ultimate downsize, a chance to be free of mortgages and other ties to the establishment. For some women, tiny homes meet ethical and

above Donna's shingle-clad home, with its generous deck, floats in a peaceful and secluded spot on Portland's Willamette River.

environmental needs, perhaps aiming to be off-grid and minimize their impact on the earth, and also to reduce their living costs.

In the waterside chapter, there are floating homes, an old duck shooting lodge turned into a holiday home, and beach huts—so ubiquitous at the British seaside—that are jolly places to be alone or with friends and family. We visited two women living in floating homes on the Willamette River in Portland, Oregon, and an Airbnb cabin, which sits in the canalside garden of an English home.

For the urban chapter, we tracked down sheds and huts in city backyards and town gardens, and made surprising finds in the spaces in between—Anita, for example, has squeezed her tiny house between a neighbor's garage and a friend's house. One woman had a shed built out of recycled materials and her friend was so impressed she had one built in her London garden too, while another had the garages at the bottom of her Brighton garden converted into music studios as a priority when she and her family moved there. We also met a young woman who wrested a shed from her father and made it a home in her parents' garden.

Out in the countryside, there is simply more room to have huts and hideaways. Here we visited hideaways in fields and woods and tucked away on smallholdings. Anne has a farm in Suffolk where students can learn how to build with straw bales, and where they have created a round house and an Owl Tower. Lindsey has the most temporary summer home and retreat when she puts up her yurt in her garden or, this year, in a field. It's an oasis for music and to get away from the farm business from time to time. On a farm in Oregon, an old hippy bus is a refuge from a music festival held on Sherry's land, and in the woods there we found the Red Dog, once an old

above Anita's tiny home has been designed to be off-grid one day and, as well as a water collection system, has solar panels.

pump house and now a sometime recording studio or retreat. You can holiday in Julie's Airstream caravan in a Norfolk paddock, or complete that novel in a writers' retreat cabin on a hill overlooking an ancient forest in the south of England.

In the Hidden chapter, we found some almost secretive places often designed to be off the beaten track, whether situated in town or country. We visited a wonderful two-story shed in Cambridge, hidden by an enthusiasm for trees, while in London we came across a shed in a community garden, its seclusion provided by a vigorous grapevine. We were allowed a special visit to a private field tucked away in Suffolk, where an extended family meet for picnics, and a coastal retreat where wildlife is abundant.

As you meander down the paths, through the garden gates, and along the byways in this book, I hope you will find inspiration for your own special hut or hideaway.

above Harriet's garden is an abundant place of flowers, herbs, fruits, and vegetables, which she preserves in her outdoor kitchen.

Chapter 1

Waterside
huts and hideaways

The desire to be close to water—whether it's days out by the river or vacations on the coast—has always been strong. There is something invigorating about "the sea air" and something calming about simply gazing out at water. Its wild nature and the constantly changing surfaces, skies, and light draw us to walk, sit, and play by the water's edge. For some, the wildlife is an ever-changing delight. For others, water features are an oasis in the rush and crush of city life. We want to be near water to feel relaxed and free from the constraints of everyday lives.

Living on houseboats or floating homes can be an answer to the challenge of city living and its sky-high property prices. This chapter features two floating homes built on huge piles, which allow the houses to rise and fall with the water and are seen as modern solutions to flooding, rising seas, and the space constraints on land.

If we can't live by water, then why not have a place to visit, such as the ubiquitous beach hut seen on so many coastal fronts in the UK? They range from those that have been in families for generations to the new wave of urban dwellers who adore the quirkiness and old-fashioned feel of the beach hut, reminding us of simpler childhoods. No twenty-first century technology—just adults and children rediscovering simply being and playing.

The women in this chapter live, play, and relax in their waterside homes and huts. They are all quite different, but have much in common in their desire to live by the water.

This beautiful old building sits on the shore of the Norfolk Broads—an extensive series of connected rivers and lakes that form one of the UK's most beautiful wetland areas. It is over one hundred years old and was probably originally a duck shooting lodge. The building has been in **Judy**'s family for several generations. Her grandparents used to sail on the Broads and when The Holt came up for sale, they would have loved to have bought it. However, it was Judy's great grandmother who purchased it, for the princely sum of £200 for the "two boys," Judy's Uncle Dick and Uncle Hugh. These days her aunt and her cousins own it. So many family memories are rooted in this place, including Judy's own wonderful childhood, and the extended family all still use this lovely isolated place. Although boats sail past throughout the summer, this area isn't nearly as busy with motorboats and tourists as some other Broads are.

It is the peace, being by the water, and the wildlife that Judy loves the most, and once a year she and her close friends spend a week here. These women are longstanding friends and are still part of a women's group started over twenty years ago. It is this intimacy of friendship and the

above The Holt, showing the beautiful thatched roof and the boathouse beyond.

opposite The wooden sailing boat "Tarka" has been here for over a hundred years.

above right Nestled into the landscape is the thatched boathouse, its doors open to the Broads.

place that are so important. Their annual week together is a chance to talk about the ups and downs of their lives. Whatever struggles they may be facing, they also have a lot of fun and laughter. Sometimes they get out onto the water in the canoe and in "Pooh," the rowing boat.

Next to The Holt are the sleeping sheds, which can accommodate up to nine people in total. On the other side of the huts is a squat, thatched boathouse where one of the oldest sailing boats on the Broads is kept—"Tarka" is about a hundred years old. Judy's women friends resist taking it out these days because it is such a palaver. The boat has to be covered with heavy planks when not in use as otters love to get in and "make havoc," Judy explains. The otters are a great success on the Broads and Judy has twice seen a large otter on the grass next to The Holt. The last time she initially thought it was a dog! She recalls, "It was absolutely enormous."

The Holt has an Edwardian feel about it, although it may have been built slightly later than this period. The furniture and fittings have hardly changed at all, with dark cupboards and shelving set against white walls, old basin stands and ornate iron hooks in some of the rooms. There is no running water or electricity. Cooking is on gas and Tilly lamps and candles provide light for card games, meals, and conversation late into the night. It is a paradise for both adults and children. Judy and her friends stay there during the "Three Rivers Race." This race has been held for over fifty years and is considered the main sailing event in the Broads calendar. They stay up all night to watch the boats go by—it's a highlight of their visit.

The open veranda gives a wonderful view of river life, including the wildlife. There are kingfishers, sedge and other warblers, swallows and marsh harriers, herons, and even cranes from time to time. Red and Chinese water deer can be spotted and cuckoos call in the spring. A treat is to see barn owls swooping across the sky, and Judy thinks there may be an owl's nest nearby along the river.

The outside walls of The Holt are treated with pitch to preserve the weatherboarding, while the thatched roof protects the building in all

weathers. Recently the whole building had to be lifted as it was gently sinking. Above the fireplace in the main room is a picture of Judy's grandfather in a boat, fully suited and wearing a hat.

In the Holt itself are two bedrooms. One is a raised double bed in a cozy alcove with a shelf for a candle or torch and hooks, but not much else. The other room has two beds and, like the main bedroom, a porcelain basin to be filled with boiled water from an old pitcher. Here very little has changed over the years. The wood burner keeps guests warm, but it can be a chilly stay without hot-water bottles.

Judy has always enjoyed the sense of being miles from anywhere and being away from the pressures of life. She shares this sense with her women friends. As well as just hanging out together, they go for long walks on the Weaver's Way to enjoy the Broads' landscape and wildlife. There is a strength in being part of a place through the generations and sharing it with her friends who have a strong and historical bond.

above One of the rustic sleeping huts with its back to the water, providing a secluded spot out of view of passing tourists.

overleaf The veranda provides the perfect place to sit on a clear day and watch the boats go by.

On England's east coast, overlooking a vast expanse of the North Sea, sit three rows of beach huts, accessed by a set of steps down from the cliff top. Across the cliff-top road there are 1920s and '30s beach houses with the distinctive architecture that differentiates nearly all seaside homes from the more serious, landlocked style found inland. In the far distance, sea-going tankers wait to dock in the huge Felixstowe docks.

As a middle-row beach-hut owner, **Jan** looks over the lower-tier roof tops, across the shingle beach, and out to this great North Sea vista. All along this weather-battered stretch of coast, banks of sea groynes hold back erosion from the relentless currents.

Jan acquired her beach hut at a price that seems very cheap compared with the cost of almost any other beach hut today, wherever it is. She says, "When I bought it, it was very run down so I was able to pay £200 ten years ago." It was painted white, but in great need of tender loving care so Jan painted it inside and out and set about making it work for her. "I brought life to it."

The sea, wind, sun, and rain take their toll on these wooden buildings. The local council also writes to owners of beach huts who don't keep them up to their standards and a letter can arrive suggesting a spruce up might be in order. Jan recently received one of these, and this was the incentive to redecorate the whole place. Once again, the inside came alive.

Jan spends as much time as she can here in the summer. The winters, she says, are miserable. She likes to arrive very early for a morning swim when no one else is about. Equally, the evenings, after the families have all gone home for their supper, are another special time when the light over the sea and the night skyscapes can be enjoyed in the midst of silence. As the voices fade at the end of the day, sometimes a friend will arrive for a game of Scrabble. A welcoming mug of tea or coffee can be brewed as the hut contains a small gas stove, while white corner cupboards store crockery and all the other essentials.

above Jan's Felixstowe beach hut is hidden in the middle of three staggered rows overlooking the North Sea.

right The doors are open to give sea views over the roof tops of the beach huts below, and the kettle is on, awaiting visitors.

"I love hearing the **sounds** of children and adults in the distance packing up ... when everyone's gone home, there is a **wonderful feeling** about the evening air and sea."

above The lines of groynes stop coastal erosion as they minimize the effect of the waves on the beaches.

opposite and inset The bare white boards and good storage leave Jan's beach hut bright and uncluttered. Open shelves display a pretty little teapot and pebbles found along the shore.

The walls of the hut are used to display children's drawings. One child has drawn both the inside and the outside of the beach hut, while another drawing shows the number of the hut. Jan loves to encourage the children to draw and tries to save them from being crumpled up or thrown away. To add contrast and a nautical feel to the hut, the bench has a blue-and-white-striped seat cushion. A matching striped curtain hides the folding chairs, which come out on sunny days.

Jan says that there is a distinctive culture among the three rows of beach huts. Many huts are held by generations of the same family and once anyone is lucky enough to get one, they are reluctant to let them go. Some owners have had their huts for the whole of their lives and many older retired people contribute to the feel of the place. It is both private and sociable.

Jan's links to this area go back years, as her father belonged to the local bowling club. As a child she hated spending time there and wanted only to be at the fairground. Now the nostalgic family connection and the fact that old Felixstowe has hardly changed are a great draw for her. Sometimes she takes the foot passenger ferry to Bawdsey and cycles across the River Deben. This is part of the Suffolk Coast Path, linking both sides of the river.

With a busy working life as a therapist, Jan always feels that she would like to spend more time here, in her little white beach hut listening to the sound of the waves, looking at the changing skies, and enjoying just being.

"When I bought the hut, it was very run down so I painted it white inside and out and brought life to it."

In the heart of England's Gloucestershire is the 200-year-old
Stroud Canal, and sitting by the canal, on a bend in the road,
is **Leah**'s Hemp Lime House and Cabin. The canal used to
join the River Severn to the River Thames in days gone by,
and restoration of the canal will, once again, link these two
great rivers.

Leah built the house herself—testament to her energy
and drive. Leah now runs her house and cabin as an Airbnb
as she likes to be able to share the good fortune she feels she
has created. Her lucky guests not only have the privilege of
staying in her hemp house or in the cabin, but they can also
stroll along the canal path into Stroud's town center.

This cabin is surprisingly spacious inside. Dark wood and
bold fabric designs could have closed the room in but the
white walls give it an airy feel. Stable doors can be left open
and the recycled windows are painted in a pale green. The
pale wooden floor and rug add to the feeling of space, and
each piece of furniture is only there if needed and placed
cleverly in the room. Beautiful cobalt blue glass lanterns add
dramatic points of color both day and night.

above and opposite Leah's Airbnb cabin is tucked against the hill, next to the path up to her self-built hemp house, which sits above the canal running along the valley in Stroud.

above Leah has an eye for a find. The sink is from a Moroccan rubbish tip and she created the colorful splashback from a mixed collection of found tiles.

opposite and inset There is plenty of space in this oddly shaped room—everything needed can be found in here, even a cozy wood burner. The decorative mirror and daylight streaming through the windows make this a bright and welcoming room.

Leah really knows how to make small spaces work. After all, for many years she lived in traveling vans and caravans before embarking on the building adventure. Her father commented to her that everywhere she lives "still looks like your caravan or the buses you've lived in."

The double bed can be folded back to make a sofa, opening up the living space for guests. The old Alba radio by the bed might look purely decorative but Leah intends to turn it into an i-pod dock and side table.

Leah has created a small table and bench where guests can sit and eat and the small kitchen area is efficient and beautiful with its unique splashback made from old tiles and glass buttons. The kitchen area contains everything needed for making coffee and tea (guests staying in the cabin can use the kitchen facilities in the house for cooking). The black tiles on the worksurface contrast and highlight the colorful splashback. Underneath are storage trays made from old apple trays and an old Marmite box.

The ornate faucet over the ceramic sink is an old garden faucet. Like many of the cabin's furnishings, the sink is a lucky find. To Leah, junkyards

from Oxfordshire to Africa are potential resources. While on vacation in Morocco, Leah spotted the sink on a rubbish dump. She has an excellent eye for the decorative, and a clear vision as to how the finds can be used.

There is an electric heater for colder days, or, more romantically, the tiny "Tortoise" wood burner can be fired up. This burner has had its own adventures—it once belonged to Leah's father who bought it for his own home, then moved it to a house in France, and, finally, gave it to Leah for the cabin. The wood burner sits against a black-tiled wall with Art Deco details and on a herringbone-patterned brick hearth.

With the canal below and the railway running behind the house, there is no chance of new building work taking away her view. The novelty of building Hemp Lime House hasn't worn off. Leah is "head over heels" in love with the house and cabin she has created. "It has me written all over it."

Oregon's Willamette River has a long and varied history, having been used for commerce and travel before the early settlers arrived and the 53,000 followers of the Oregon Trail opened up this part of the west coast. At this time the river lazily wound its way around islands until dredging and clearing created the wide, deep river we see in Portland today.

There was a time when the river was full of ocean-going ships, paddle steamers, and every other kind of boat needed in the early development of cities and towns, such as Portland and Eugene. Industry built up along the river, with the waste from those industries being dumped directly into the river. The inevitable result was that the water became neglected and polluted. It wasn't until after the Second World War that improvements were made and the river began to recover. In 1967 the Willamette River Greenway program finally enabled the river to be cleaned up. It is in this clean river that floating home moorings have sprung up, some of them gated communities with very expensive properties.

Pam's floating house is not in a gated compound; rather, it is one of about thirty or so homes of all sizes reached by a steep ramp from the bank to this small community. It is a hideaway in the sense that it is totally unseen from the road above and is an oasis of water, trees, and wildlife in the thriving city. Pam says, "It's not exactly a hideaway in the summer when curious tourists come down to have a look!" Nevertheless, it is a respite of tranquility from city life.

The range of accommodation varies from the grand to smaller, more hut-like homes. Architectural styles and materials make this a fascinating place. The floating homes rest on a network of logs, stringers, shims, pins, flotation, and chaining attached to the mooring slip. Massive piles driven into the river bed support this network and allow the houses to rise and fall with water levels.

above The first things you notice about Pam's floating home are the bright splashes of color and glitter on the deck.

opposite Pam's home viewed from the steep ramp leading down to this floating community.

Pam's floating home is one of the oldest on the river, probably built in the 1930s. She has lived here for many years and has created a beautiful home that combines period features and furniture with a love for color. Outside, the walls are clad with soft gray weatherboarding with white trims, and pots of plants surround the floating home. The iron pillars holding up the roof at the front of the home are painted purple to match the window awnings and seats.

At the end of the deck facing the shore is a planted-up area with a bright pink parasol and another seating area.

above The traditional sitting room with its dark wood paneling is brightened up with Pam's "leopardskin" lampshade —one of her own designs.

opposite Trees and shrubs in containers soften the timber-clad walls. The bowed window has a copper roof to match the copper-covered curved roof.

inset Two cushioned chairs beneath a sculpted three-mast ship provide one of the many seating areas on the deck.

The interior suggests an Edwardian feel with the dark furniture, and Pam's love of lamps and lamp design adds to the rich, sumptuous interior style. She has designed many of the lamps herself, with one lamp displaying her penchant for leopardskin patterning. The bathroom still has the original features painted white but with a modern glass basin and waterfall faucet. Above this is a stained-glass window depicting a mermaid, which ties in with Pam's email name.

Pam's home even includes a bar with a purple chandelier, which faces on to the deck with the parasol. Here, outside the bar, is some privacy. Even so, anyone coming down the access ramp will enjoy a clear view of her home, including the new copper roof. It is from this deck that Pam can enjoy the wildlife, particularly the ducks. They come on board and she has adopted a favorite, Squirt, who will come into the home to see her.

A piece of furniture that has great meaning for Pam is an old rocking chair that belonged to her grandmother. She is a descendant of one of the families who reached Oregon on the great Oregon Trail. Times have been hard for Pam with tragic loss and illness and, at one time, she wanted to leave the floating home. However, circumstances have changed and she now says she will stay. She loves to have her grandchildren visit and designates chairs on the deck for just them.

"I decided to stay here and I am **glad** I did, as it is a great place for the **grandchildren** to come and visit me."

Several years ago **Elly** had an accident and broke her back, with the result that she had to leave a rewarding job in London and rethink how she and her son, Charlie, would live. Until then, she had been a classic London visitor, coming down to Brighton year after year and loving it. An important silver lining presented itself when Elly realized she could live in Brighton full time and buy a beach hut.

A clear vision emerged. She and Charlie moved to a top-floor apartment in town, and Elly prioritized her search for a beach hut. As luck would have it, she managed to find one that wasn't near the most touristy and busy part of the sea front. Her hut is one of a long, long line of color on Brighton sea front. It isn't large but with a claimed patch designated by a pink and orange plastic mat, brightly colored chairs, and a windbreak made from a jolly Ikea fabric, this outside room setting gives Elly all the space she needs. In the winter she can feel "tucked in and warm" and in the summer it provides "shade and sanity."

The hut is now kitted out in the retro style Elly adores. To complement the bright blues of the doors, bunting hangs on the back wall, and solar lights provide sparkle at night. The hut contains the most amazing amount of stuff, including swing ball and skates, all suspended from the roof in netting.

The hut is now a huge part of her and her son's lives. They come down early, swim on some days, and once a week they bike down, swim, cook breakfast, and then he goes to school while she gets on with her day, which includes working part-time. Sometimes Elly makes hot chocolate and takes a nap in the afternoon. After school, they bike down again

above Elly and her son cycle down from their apartment to the beach hut, where a pink and orange mat can be placed outside to claim an outdoor sitting area.

right Elly's view from the hut is across the wide Brighton promenade and onward to the sea, where she loves to take an early morning swim.

to the front and can easily spend three or four hours in the hut and on the beach, with a quick and easy beach-hut supper of pasta or baked beans on toast. Elly says, "It's my garden."

If Elly is on the beach, she puts out a notice for visitors. She can be easily spotted in her 1950s swimming costumes and bright 1950s swimming hats, which she has enhanced with extra-large colorful flowers. She describes herself as a sea bather from April to October. One way or another, the hut is used all year round. In the winter they get down to the front twice a week or so and they have had two Christmas lunches there. Cup-a-Soups, hot chocolate, a wine cooler, and seven varieties of tea are part of the kit for all occasions.

Elly also enjoys her own company. If she feels the need for privacy, the clues will all be there. Only one chair is out; there is no notice that she might be on the beach; the doors might be shut. By contrast, at other times she has had huge dinner parties for up to twelve people. There really are enough tables and chairs in this small beach hut to cater for many guests. How, one wonders, does she do it? She is, she admits, a storage fanatic and uses every inch of the hut without making it look cluttered. She is very particular about how everything that comes out of the hut goes back. It's a Tardis. There is even a barbecue and a skateboard hidden under the turquoise-and-green striped bench. In one storm her beach hut was one of the few that remained upright. Elly joked that it was because of all the stuff holding it down!

Ultimately this little beach hut meets a huge amount of Elly's needs and those of her son. There is privacy and there is sociability, there is the beach and the sea, and a place to express her 1950s style preferences. She says of the hut, "It has completely changed our lives. It's my social life. I am tied to Brighton by the hut. It helps us with our health and happiness. It's my family space and my private space."

above Elly loves the retro life and wears 1950s swimming costumes and swimming hats, which she enhances with additional bright flowers.

opposite If the doors are open, the mat is laid down, and there is more than one chair put out, then friends are welcome to call in.

overleaf Elly opens the doors and claims her colorful space amongst a long line of Brighton beach huts.

"The hut has **completely** changed our lives. It's my
social life, it helps us with our **health** and **happiness**.
It's my family space and my private space."

Donna has been living in her riverside floating community for over twenty three years. Such a long stay wasn't intended, nor was the move to Portland, Oregon as she didn't have any previous ties to the city. It was purely the location that drew her here.

The mooring on the Willamette River—a major tributary of the Columbia River—is accessible only by an obscure entrance. As you approach through the mature trees, the river opens up in front of you and far below, the floating homes are laid out with wooden boardwalks linking them to each other and to the steep ramp that runs down the hill. The inhabitants here get used to pushing wheelbarrows laden with all the heavier day-to-day items up and down this incline.

Donna had reached a stage in her life where her children had grown and become independent, allowing her to tick off one of her "bucket list" wishes of living on the water. She was considering moving to Seattle, but a friend told her about the Willamette River property and she was hooked. When Donna first rented the place, she began to fall in love with it so, when the opportunity arose, she bought the shingle-clad home ,which consists of two separate huts, even though they were in poor repair at the time.

opposite Donna's shingle-clad home has a large deck with an awning and her lush planting, which creates her outdoor living space.

right Unless seen from above, Donna's floating home, facing the beach, is slightly hidden by the plants on the deck.

"I was thinking of moving, perhaps to Seattle, but a friend showed me this house so I rented it for a while to try it out. There is something cathartic about the water and I couldn't wait to buy it."

"I am a homebody who doesn't need the city of Portland ... this is the tranquil place I love."

above Donna's home comprises two buildings. The second "hut" is Donna's bedroom and bathroom and backs onto the boardwalk.

The house was originally sited on the Columbia River, before being towed to this pretty spot nestling beneath the busy city and roads. It is one of the oldest houses on the river still floating on giant logs attached to the huge piles, which both anchor the floating homes and allow them to rise and fall with the water. Donna explains that the visible giant logs hide a system of "sister" logs to support the building. Some floating homes have had to be repaired and now have additional modern floats of concrete and Styrofoam to support them as old timbers rot or sag.

The home now has a bedroom and a bathroom in the rear hut and a studio/sitting room at the front with large glass doors. When they are fully open, this creates a wonderfully light indoor/outdoor space. During the warmer months of the year, Donna mostly lives on the deck, spending as much time outside as the weather allows her to. Here are seats, a comfortable lounger, and tables, with privacy provided by a living screen of planted willows which sway in the breeze. On the other side is a copper privacy fence covered in green vines to soften them and make them more enjoyable for the near neighbors, too.

To reach this semi-secluded deck, visitors walk along the side of the shingle huts before arriving at a plant-filled space with the view of the shore. As well as tall willows and bamboos, Donna has an array of colorful pots filled with flowers, including canna lilies and lantana. Bright red crocosmia are set off by black mondo grass. In the winter, the landscape loses its

greenery and the flowers die off, but the jolly pots and some ceramic bird boxes remain to add interest.

There are two sides to the boardwalk "street," and the homes nearer the shore have less movement from the waves created by passing boats. These homes also enjoy a view of the beach, the trees, and other vegetation. The local wildlife is a bonus, although the geese are considered a nuisance as they make a mess on the floating gardens. Donna has spotted otters, deer, ducks, and many species of birds. She has seen nutria (also known as coypu) and, soaring above the river, bald eagles. She says there is something cathartic about the water.

Living in such a small and manageable home allows Donna to indulge her love of travel. Sitting on the deck, she can contemplate, read, think, and plan her next traveling adventure.

above Donna has a view down the Willamette River and of the shore, perfect for watching the wildlife while planning her travels.

Ivy lives by the Willamette River in Portland, Oregon, and has a prime view of St John's Bridge with its extraordinary cathedral-like design. It was a surprise and an intrigue to find that we were close to the river. Through a meandering semi-wilderness behind the main house you can see the view, and a little further along a winding path stands the Mud Hut.

Ivy bought her property because of its location. She wanted her own land, so bought the house and started dreaming. The Mud Hut was originally conceived as a fire pit and sauna, so it began as a sunken room, accessed by crawling through a low door and down some steps. There would be benches all around and a central fire pit for hot stones. The end result, however, was not the egg-shaped sauna of Ivy's dreams.

Ivy originally envisaged a floor spiral made of stones and shells. The walls would be sculptural and flowing with a snake design—for Ivy, this represents a creature of transformation and healing. Many of the stones came from the banks of the nearby Columbia River Gorge. Ivy collected the crystals herself from a place of childhood memory—Crystal Peak in California. She recalls the exhilarating, magical feeling of clarification and cleansing as she stood on the quartz mountain.

As she and her friends, family, and community began to dig downward and create the footprint for the Mud Hut, it simultaneously grew outward, with a bigger diameter than intended. Never mind, they thought—they would build upward bit by bit until they reached the half-wall height Ivy was looking for. The walls were designed to be thick

opposite The pink mud hut was to have been a sauna, but it grew into a meeting place for Ivy and her women friends, and then became an Airbnb, allowing others to learn about and enjoy the building.

right Ivy's Mud Hut has a view of St John's Bridge, with its "cathedral" arches, just down river.

"I wanted a place where I could have enough land to build in cob ... so I bought this house and started dreaming of a sauna shaped like an egg, but it became something else."

top Glimpses of the spiral floor, the benches, and the snake decoration around the walls are reminders that the Mud Hut is a meeting place as well as somewhere to stay.

above After dusk there are candles to be lit, and candle niches have been sculpted into the walls.

and, as such, have a great thermal mass, keeping the space warm in the winter and cool in the summer. The walls approached the height she envisioned and then, with the wider diameter, first one person and then another wondered what it would be like if they continued to build the walls up to full height. It seemed that the proportions of the building were asking to change. It might have other purposes as well as being a sauna. So they followed their instincts and kept building. The result is the Mud Hut we see today.

Much of the building materials were upcycled, including the very long log which makes the central beam of the leaf-shaped roof. It was found on the shore of the river and it was quite a struggle to get it up the hill. Other materials were found on Craigslist, a website well used by those in search of recycled and secondhand items. The whole process was quite organic and Ivy says, "We made it up as we went along." It took three good summers to complete. Ivy hosted a mosaic workshop where participants joined in making the mirrored mosaic at the top of the wall. It sparkles and reflects light in this cave-like space. The walls were painted with clay paints and natural pigments of ocher and a soft pink. Gothic arches reflect the gothic arches of St John's Bridge. The floor is inlaid with stones, shells, and crystals, received as gifts from others and gathered on Ivy's own travels.

As the floor is sunken, they created a moisture barrier but left the very center of the spiral open to let the building breath. Ivy also realized that people felt unsafe with a central open fire, so she was able to source an old collectable Dutch woodstove, called a Squirrel Stove.

For seven years Ivy has used the hut for ritual and celebration with her close women friends. She feels a deep attachment to this space as her two children were born here. Recently the women dedicated the hut as a temple to magic and the spaces in-between. As time went by, Ivy realized that there was another way to share her hut and began taking in Airbnb guests. These tended to be young couples and those interested in the techniques used to build it. She and her partner, whom she met while building, made a removable double bed so they wouldn't lose the sauna and celebratory space and soon it was ready to welcome guests.

The building is topped with a green roof shaped like a leaf, with the long pole found on the river bank as the center of the leaf. The point of the leaf protrudes, creating shelter over the door. Outside, Ivy created a semi-open cubicle from salvaged windows and wood panels where women can change before entering the hut when they have a sauna. The cubicle floor is studded with shells collected locally or brought by friends.

Although there are houses around and buildings far below on the hill, the hut is unseen and a place where Ivy feels protected. There are times when the space reverts back to a personal retreat where Ivy can relax for a while and take a nap with the door open. She sees a time when she might reclaim it from Airbnb. In the meantime, it is a place to inspire and educate and to share with her community. As she says, "The thing I dreamt about having in my life is, as I look about, in my life right now ... It's a gift that keeps giving."

above An efficient wood burner, which replaced a central fire pit, takes the chill off the night air.

Mary's beach hut is on England's north Norfolk coast, one of a long row of colorful huts on stilts looking out to the North Sea. The beach is long and sandy and extremely popular both with walkers all year around and with "residents" and visitors in summer. Behind the huts are wooded dunes, and beyond them a café and a path to the local seaside town.

The distance to the sea, over an inlet, gives the impression of a steely blue line with flashes of white wave tops and an occasional white sail tacking along the coast. For Mary, her pre-breakfast swims mean a longish walk across the sand before a cold but refreshing dip. Only then can a cooked breakfast be the reward!

A beach hut had long been on Mary's wish list. When she investigated the possibility of buying one, there were three for sale. So she submitted her bids and went away on vacation. She was very, very lucky to have her bid accepted for this one, not because it

above left From the steps over the dunes, beyond the pale blue hut, the vast beach and the North Sea horizon can be seen.

above Mary's beach hut is the base for big summertime family get-togethers, with cricket and swims, picnics and naps.

opposite From the inside you can look out over the veranda to the sea. Towels hang ready for the those who brave the long walk across the beach to swim in the cold North Sea.

was the most beautiful, but because it had a wide veranda and, at that time, she could use the whole footprint to build a larger beach hut. She got in at a good time—building regulations are now far stricter and 6 x 8-foot (1.8 x 2.4-m) sheds are the maximum allowed these days. Her plot is also next to the steps leading up to the communal wash house and loos.

Mary employed a builder who had constructed many of the huts on this stretch of beach and he built it to her own design. She mentioned to him that she would ideally like a bed but added that she knew sleeping in the huts at night is not allowed, so he created two daybeds—a long, fold-out bench on one side and another single bed hinged to the other side. On rainy days the single can be set up and friends and family can still enjoy being at the beach. For sunnier days, there are folding chairs, hats and towels, blankets and rugs for the beach. The floor has a grass mat, which is easy to shake out.

Mary filled in the space above the veranda for storage, and had a porthole made where her teddy can sit and look out to sea. The beach hut is aptly called the "Bear Hut." When Mary is in, a wooden seagull is placed on the roof to show she is "in residence."

The hut is reached up a flight of stairs onto the veranda, which is decorated with colorful bunting. The interior shows the natural wood-paneled structure and the long bench is covered with a bright stripey cloth. Deciding on the color scheme, decorating, making the interior beautiful, and buying such essentials as the jolly crockery was a true pleasure. That year Mary had "such a happy summer."

After her hut was finished, Mary soon met Daphne and Bill, who had owned their beach hut for fifty years. Mary says they taught her all she needed to know about successful "hutting," the key to which is to get up early and put out your windbreak to claim the beach in front of your hut. Sadly, Daphne and Bill are no longer there, but fond memories linger on.

Mary was raised by the sea, so acquiring a beach hut feels like a real achievement. She doesn't feel the need to get away from her everyday life—it's a good one—but she does love the occasional opportunity to spend some time alone. Whether the beach is deserted in the winter and very, very quiet or thronging with children in the summer, she loves it. "It's magical to feel part of the sea and the sky." Getting up early for a swim in the sea is one of her special treats and the vast skies and sands are wonderful.

Although she enjoys time spent on her own, Mary also loves sharing the hut with her family, so children and grandchildren come down for the day to swim, play cricket, have picnics, and enjoy the freedom being on the beach gives young children. Mary also receives beach visits from close friends she met at relaxation class as the women like to meet up at the hut from time to time.

Lunch is set out on a table on the sand and everyone can help themselves to sandwiches and salads. Mary has a gas hob in the shed so that coffee and tea can be offered, perhaps followed by an afternoon doze for some of the adult visitors!

above Steep wooden steps lead to the veranda. Above the veranda, sitting in a porthole, is the teddy bear after which the hut is named. When Mary is there, she puts a wooden seagull on the roof to show she is in residence.

Chapter 2
Countryside
huts and hideaways

While urban huts and hideaways might present space issues, there is usually more room in the countryside, maybe more scope for doing up outbuildings, as Canny did for her herbalism business, or for building more substantial sheds, or for an Airstream to take root in the paddock—here, the USA has come to the English countryside in the guise of an Airstream caravan gleaming beneath sun-dappled leaves in the deepest countryside.

Also in this chapter, Lindsey puts up her hideaway yurt in a field in front of her house each summer to play music, sleep outdoors, and get away from the farm business. Marie and her partner run a wonderful eco-campsite and a pub, so her peaceful getaway is a hut on wheels, built with recycled materials and love.

Dom's shed, which she constructed herself, is a many splendored thing with a variety of uses, while Monica's cabin on the hill was once a yoga retreat but now has a second life as a fabulous writers' retreat for women.

Some hideaways, such as Anne's straw-bale roundhouse, have the wonder of being set in wide landscapes that change according to the light, the seasons, the colors, and the wildlife. Anne's storytelling hut is part of the landscape and, as with the other huts and hideaways in this chapter, helps us connect with nature and ourselves.

"We'll take off the old corrugated tin walls on the
stables and I want lots of glass. Will it be too posh?"

Canny lives down a long and bumpy track on the edge of an ancient village green in Suffolk. She and her partner have lived there since the 1970s, in the days when people could buy dilapidated old farmhouses for very little money if they had the vision to renovate and, often, rebuild them. In those days the roof might be open to the skies and pigs might be running through the ground-floor rooms, but the early adventurers would come up from London to peer through dust and cobwebs into untouched rooms where farmers of old once lived with their families.

Canny and Keith bought their cottage in an auction. The lot also included stables for Canny's horses, and the barns where the reeds for Keith's thatching work are stacked high.

Canny also needed a space for her silver jewelry-making work, so she took over a dilapidated shed which leant against one of the barns. One end had completely fallen down, so Canny set about rebuilding, not knowing that she was pregnant at the time as she re-felted and tiled the roof. She rebuilt the end wall and put down a screed to level the floor. Unfortunately, although she insulated the walls and ceiling, she didn't insulate the floor so the cold would rise and bring a chill to the room.

opposite Canny's shed is a converted lean-to and is part of the original Suffolk farm barns and outbuildings.

left One of the shed walls had to be completely rebuilt as it had collapsed. It is clad with traditional weatherboarding painted black.

Canny painted the walls and ceilings off-white to draw as much light into the interior as possible. Practical worktables and shelves and a mid-twentieth century kitchen unit completed the room. The rebuilt wall features an attractive mullion window that she made herself. She calls it a "bodge" mullion but had she not said, it would be impossible to tell it's not a professional job. Canny re-used the existing beams and added a Georgian stable door to open out on to the beautiful cottage garden. The outside of the shed melds with the barn behind it, as they are all clad in traditional black weatherboarding.

After working for some years as a jeweler, Canny revisited a childhood dream. She loved plants from an early age and as a child made "potions" of lavender heads steeped in water to sell to friends. Her mother was a great gardener and an inspiration to her. It was being surrounded by plants growing wild and "doing their own thing" that inspired Canny to become a herbalist. And so she studied and began to make her own mixtures, tinctures, and lotions. She invested time and money in gaining the relevant qualifications, and in business and marketing training, but over time the herbalists' trade became much harder as the red tape, rules, and regulations increasingly tightened their grip on this ancient knowledge and craft. For Canny, the joy was being squeezed out of the business, so she decided to stop seeing clients and now treats friends and family only.

The shed now also houses a bench on one side where Canny has started to make stained glass as it's too messy and dangerous to do in the house. She needs another studio, and so has her vision set on some other outbuildings on their land. Sadly, the last of her horses has now gone and the two stables stand empty. One of these will be her new space to be creative—to design and make stained glass safely, to sing and to dance.

above Canny uses the mid-century cabinet and the shelves above the workbench as storage for her herbal medicines, which she prescribes just for friends and family these days.

opposite For the rebuilt shed wall, Canny made a "bodged" mullion window.

And so these eighteenth-century stables and barns have been given a new role, one that combines function as well as beauty. The stables are built of clay lump—a cob-like local material. The front of the stable currently has a corrugated metal wall, but this will be removed to make way for a large glass window. Roof lights will help make this dream of space and light come true.

"My mother was a great gardener. I always loved herbs and, as a child, I collected plants ... and started making potions, such as lavender heads in water, and selling them."

Canny likes the idea of covering the floor with rubber horse matting, which interlocks and is warm under the feet, and adding a wood burner. It is a mixture of longing for the new, yet not being under any time pressure—it will be when it will be.

Even before the arrival of her Airstream Safari, **Julie** had already constructed one hideaway on her land in Norfolk. She had built The Cob House, an earth and straw house which is used by groups and friends as a welcoming space for all kinds of activities. Many a drum has been played into the night with only the moon, stars, and candlelight to see by.

The American addition to this lovely wooded corner in a Norfolk paddock came about in the last two years. When Julie talked about opening a B&B business in her Norfolk home, a friend made the intriguing suggestion of buying an Airstream caravan to provide extra accommodation for guests. Through friends of friends, Julie found a contact in the USA who exports these iconic aluminum caravans. What started as a whim became an exciting reality when Julie bought this 1955 Airstream Safari.

The Airstream was shipped across the Atlantic to Southampton and then transported north to Yorkshire for renovation. The Airstream was in a poor condition and the wheels didn't work so it was put onto a low loader for the next phase of its journey.

Once the refurbishment was complete, the final stage was to get the Airstream in place. It had to be moved up a track, then into the paddock, and finally placed in the shady area in the far corner on Julie's land. A tractor was brought in and, finally, this gleaming

opposite Julie's Airstream caravan was transported from the USA and had a trip to the north of England for renovation, before ending up in this wooded paddock for guests to enjoy.

right To keep the shine on the caravan, from time to time Julie gives it a jet wash and a rub down with a soft cloth and flour so there are no scratches.

addition to the paddock was settled in the bluebell wood. In the sunshine the trees are reflected in the curves of the aluminum, while the sunlight falling through the canopy creates a wonderful dappled effect, adding to the play of light and shade on and around the Airstream.

During its renovation, the aluminum exterior was taken back to a gleaming shine. Julie told me that to restore the finish now that it sits in the field, a jet wash followed by a rub down with a soft cloth and flour does the trick, keeping the shine and preventing scratches.

The interior was refitted in 1950s style using pale wood veneers. The original veneers would probably have been darker, but Julie chose a lighter finish to add a modern touch without sacrificing the retro look. The table has a soft gray melamine inset and the practical lino flooring picks up the same gray tones. Julie has added a few period finishing touches—a vintage 1950s tray, a pink retro radio, an enamel ice-cream advertising panel, and two retro cookbooks for guests to browse while deciding what to cook in the neat kitchen area.

The double bed is at one end of the caravan, with cabinets on each side and above. The table and benches convert into a child's bed and Julie allows

camping in the wood if there are more children than beds. If guests leave the gate in the picket fence open, dogs from the house visit and make friends with anyone who will have them. They, too, welcome those who come to this shaded retreat to get away from the city or to celebrate special occasions in this bygone world.

The Airstream has all mod cons, although there is no phone signal or internet connection, which is hard for some and a delight for others. However, the games cupboard above the bed is explored and games from childhood are rediscovered and taught to the next generation. With the lack of technology, here is both disconnection from outside distractions and reconnection with loved ones. On rainy days the Airstream is a cocoon and a haven.

There is a rustic bucket loo nearby for the brave, in a shelter constructed from hazel with a pretty timber door!

Julie has turned this piece of history into a quirky B&B for romantic retreats and family holidays for those wanting to tour Norfolk and Suffolk. The local pub has also proved very popular with guests and walks can include a visit to the remains of a castle on the edge of this village. When we visited Julie, the spring bluebells were carpeting the ground. In the fall, she says, crab apples drop from the trees above and bounce off the roof, landing with a thud on the ground.

above The retro-fitting of the interior includes all mod cons, except phone signal and internet access, so the experience of staying here reflects truly another, simpler time.

58 countryside huts and hideaways

above The straw-bale Storytelling Hut is in the style of an African rondavel.

opposite left and right The classroom was the first straw-bale building Anne and Barbara made with students—a timber frame with bale infill. It is here that they run courses in many kinds of countryside skills and pursuits.

Anne lives with her husband, Bob, in Suffolk on a beautiful hilly organic farm spread over 70 acres with its own lake and set in its own valley. Assington Mill has numerous outbuildings which blend with the main house and the surroundings perfectly. They look as though they have been there forever, but they are relatively new straw-bale buildings constructed by Anne with Barbara Jones, who started Amazon Nails in 1980. Amazon Nails was originally a women's roofing company until Barbara fell in love with straw-bale building, at which point her business changed direction and it is now called Straw Works.

These two women work using straw-bale building techniques and teach these easily accessible methods to students who want to learn how to construct affordable and sustainable buildings. Anne has been able to get the local authority to support this enterprise since they build for educational purposes.

The first building they created was a large classroom. After getting planning permission for it, twenty-four people came to learn and build. This building was designed as a timber-framed structure with straw-bale infill, using straw and clay from the land. They have left a straw bale on view for students and a triangle under one of the windows is "signed" by many hands in clay. A mixture of clay, chopped straw, cow muck, and water was mixed by the fun process of students treading it together, with many feet needed to get just the right consistency. The render is a finer mix, requiring two or three coats, with a final layer of a light ocher slip. Anne comments that it is difficult to go wrong—the technique seems to be "just chuck it in."

On the farm the students construct real buildings that have a purpose, such as the Storytelling Hut. This is a round thatched building with low walls, and inside you can look up at the pattern of the hazel ceiling, supported by round poles. The foundations are made from a layer of old car tires on rammed chalk. The base and top of the straw bales have shaped wall plates, and then three layers of bale make up the low walls.

Anne says that they were lucky to find a young thatcher, who was in the process of getting his Master Thatcher certificate, to create the thick thatch. The high land, the thick thatch overhang, and the car tire foundations make this a very sound building which should last for many years.

The curved benches were handmade to fit against the walls. A four-legged fire bowl sits in the center and, when only the embers remain, the stories can begin. Late at night, with the flames flickering and a breeze wafting through the open door, the tales have an added atmospheric charge.

The natural ocher interior adds to the earthy sense of this building. The thatched roof hangs low over the doorway and the whole place has the feel of an African rondavel, especially when seen from afar, half-hidden by long grass and with the huge Suffolk sky above. A large swing seat perched on a rise next to the farmhouse provides a perfect view of the hut and the surrounding fields and woods.

Along a mown path through the fields and along a rough path near a stream there is a gate. The view from that wooden farm gate, to the other

above At night, with the embers of the fire to provide warmth and a breeze from the open door, storytelling becomes magical and atmospheric for those sitting on the benches lining the walls.

above right The hazel and reed thatched roof is very thick and weatherproof, and will last for many years.

end of a long wild meadow, takes in the Owl Tower, which looks completely natural against the hay and wild flowers with its backdrop of trees moving gently in the wind. The Owl Tower was built in 2008—Anne wanted to demonstrate that she could build a two-story cob structure. This building was originally intended for human use on the ground level, but that has not happened, and the owls have this luxury tower to themselves. The males and females have separate boxes in the apex of the tower. Baby owls flap around, practising flying from joist to joist inside before taking off into the wild as adults. Fifteen chicks have fledged so far. Anne calls it "an owl palace."

The most recent student building project was the Cart Lodge, constructed in 2011. This now houses old farm machinery, and two pairs of swallows have taken up residence there.

Anne runs courses all year round, except in August and December. As well as cob building, they run workshops in the classroom on traditional and rural skills, such as bee-keeping, soap-making, and much more. People staying in the guest accommodation can take part in any of these activities or just enjoy their surroundings.

The large mill wheel next to the guest cottages no longer works, but the name of the business—Assington Mill Rural Skills and Craft Courses—reminds us of its origins.

above The Owl Tower, in a meadow by a stream, may initially have been intended for a human purpose, but it has turned out to be an "owl palace" for the lucky owls.

Monica runs a retreat for women writers in Forest Row, East Sussex. They come here to finish novels, work to deadlines, wait for inspiration, and escape from the everyday distractions that can get in the way of the creative process.

Monica is a writer and has also worked as a radio producer, journalist, and psychotherapist. She now runs writing workshops and it is these experiences that draw her to explore writing as a process. She explains, "Drawing from my notebooks, prose, poetry, and dramatic dialogues, I write a blog showing how writing can be experienced and explored. The issues tackled are those that affect us all: love, anger, and sadness; the joys and difficulties of relationships; illness, happiness, and spirituality. Using a wide range of literary styles, my examples will help the reader to experience the creative and healing potential of writing for well-being."

Behind her traditional red brick and tiled house, there is a steep garden with vegetable plots and flower beds, where strawberries and raspberries glint jewel-like through fruit trees and tumble over low brick walls. Summer flowers include crocosmia, lavenders, alliums, sweet williams, peonies, and nasturtiums, plus an abundance of herbs. There are seating areas for contemplation of the view over the top of the house to Ashdown Forest, which was enclosed as a royal hunting park in the thirteenth century.

left Guests can sit at the desk, with a view over Ashdown Forest, and wait for inspiration, enjoying the time and space to think and write.

overleaf The cabin sits in a peaceful and secluded spot at the very top of Monica's steep garden.

The cabin at the top of her garden was originally built by Monica's then husband as a yoga space, but now it has a new life for, in Monica's words, "those who need time away from busy lives to focus on maybe a novel, poems, or a project that needs time out and attention." The steep hill and path up to the cabin give it its name, "The Cabin on the Hill." Behind the building, mature oak trees frame the cabin with their rich summer foliage. There are many spaces for resting, eating, or waiting for inspiration.

Monica's own writing room is in the house. She has stayed up on the hill when there have been family parties and her family have also used it from time to time, but it has another life as a place where women come for between two and five days to write. Monica keeps costs as low as possible to support aspiring and established writers and they can stay according to their own rhythms and needs.

Exterior wavy-edged cedar cladding gives the cabin the appearance of being rustic, but this belies the comfort to be found inside this simple one-room space. Monica says, "Many have described the ambience as a magical space." The guest book is filled with phrases such as "completely at ease," another felt "calm and composed," and a third writer described her mood as one of "blissful concentration."

Guests can be as independent as they choose. The cabin has a small stove and wood burner for heat. There is a sofa-bed and the all-important writing table faces the window with a view. The wall behind the wood burner is lined with slate, while other walls are cedar-clad, giving the air of a log cabin. Guests don't have far to go to fetch logs and the sympathetically built lean-to log shed just outside is neatly stacked with winter wood. The cabin can be used all year round—the wood burner and insulation make it very cozy. Monica even says it is warmer than the main house in winter! The decor is uncluttered but charming. In the summer the windows and doors can be flung open to experience the expansive view of Ashdown Forest.

Monica explains, "Breakfasts and simple meals can be prepared in the cabin and eaten at any time to suit early and late risers. Some

guests enjoy their evening meal arriving on a tray, while others like to eat with me at the kitchen table in the house. This is the sort of hospitality I would enjoy for myself on retreat—one of great flexibility according to each day's needs."

She continues, "The essential element of a writing retreat is that sense of being alone with your writing and the obvious advantage of solitude. Nevertheless, being on your own can present a challenge for those who have never been on retreat before, but I've been told it is reassuring to know that I'm an invisible presence at the bottom of the garden." That Monica is a writer too gives some women the sense of being understood and supported in ways they might not experience in other retreats.

Monica says she has a "catholic" sense of hospitality and providing a space for women also fulfills her feminist aims. "This is small scale ... but I can offer my house and cabin to women writers. In today's increasingly busy world, it is hard to find time alone and particularly time without activity and demands. And time with silence."

above The cabin is simply and tastefully furnished. The rear wall is clad with cedar paneling, with slate tiles behind the wood burner. Rugs, throws, natural woods, and an old rustic door add to the feeling of warmth and welcome.

above Dom has built many houses and this one is her storage shed and private space when she needs to be away from the bustle and sociability of those living around her.

opposite The kitchen area is a pleasing jumble of equipment and belongings that remind Dom of family and friends.

inset In a corner of the kitchen is a photo of Dom's husband Pete's mother and aunt. He died a few years ago and this photo is a fond link to this lovely man.

Dom lives as part of a community in Norfolk. Like her father before her, she is a builder and the houses and outbuildings in this place are testament to her skills. The mix of family and other people living in and around the community means it is a lively and busy environment. At the moment Dom shares her own house with tenants, so she needed another place to retreat to when she feels like time to herself.

The "bones" of this shed build are a timber frame with a pantiled roof. The floor has been recycled from an old pine floor unearthed among Dom's father's many stacks of wood. Her father Selwyn was an avid recycler and rescuer of old building materials (see page 202). When he was converting maltings in Diss, he used beautiful oak floors rescued from an old pub in nearby Kenninghall. Some of the leftover oak was used by Dom's brother in sheds he was building (see page 166), while Dom used the rest to clad the interior walls of her own storage shed. Like so many shed builders, old and new finds and recycling are part of the ethos of creating individual spaces that reflect long-held ideals.

Downstairs is a motley mixture of tables, chests, and shelves, some of which make up the kitchen area. None of it is formal and it is full of bits and pieces from old friends and from the family. A photo of her husband Pete's mother and aunt reminds Dom of them and connects her to Pete, who died not so long ago, and there are other reminders of this lovely man, such as a picture of his guru in the sleeping loft upstairs and his guitar leaning against a wall.

left The sleeping mezzanine provides a comfortable bed for the occasional guest.

far left At the top of the stairs an unusual banister is a reminder of childhood as it formed part of her parents' French-style bed many years ago.

below left Dom follows the "anti-design" ethos of her builder father, but combines it with a love of beautiful things. On the table is a sculpted head made by her son.

below The outside shower, made from recycled materials, has a view across the fields.

Dom explains that local planning regulations do not allow this shed to be used as a permanent home, so it has a mixture of uses. It's her study and guest room, and storage room for all those meaningful things acquired over the years. The shed has also served as a studio and two sculpted heads made by her son sit on one of the tables. There are lots of paintings stored here, some by Pete. There are too many to hang on the walls and Dom wonders what to do with this art collection.

The sleeping loft is basic but comfortable, while the rest of the shed is open to the roof. The unusual banister at the top of the steep open stairs is the last remaining part of her parents' beautifully curved bedhead, salvaged and put to new use. Dom remembers the large French-style bed from her childhood, and this is a touching link to the past. The recycling theme continues behind the shed, where there is a shower lined with tiles painted by Peter Davis, a local potter.

Dom's storage shed is her place, where she doesn't have to clean, where she can leave a mess, and do whatever she likes without judgment. She adds, "The voles come in from the surrounding fields and announce their presence with their scratching."

Dom's father was anti-interior design and had an "aversion to the bourgeoisie." Although she has followed in his building footsteps, Dom admits to liking beautiful things and pictures and color, with a measure of anti-design thrown in. With these traits, values, and heritage from strong family ties, Dom recognizes Selwyn's essential role in enabling her to be who she is and achieve her building dreams.

"George loves it now, but really it's my space.
It was really worth the investment. When he goes
away, I move in here with Ry, the dog."

above Each summer Lindsey erects her yurt in the garden.

above right The table to eat at and the balafon to play music on reflect Lindsey's love of entertaining.

Each summer, as soon as the weather allows, **Lindsey** puts up her yurt on the farm she and George live on in Suffolk and there it stays until summer moves into fall, at which point it is stored away again until the next year.

Lindsey and George live in a small cottage surrounded by farm buildings and tree-lined fields of cows. They work for themselves, exporting farm equipment, and the house also serves as their office.

A friend recommended that Lindsey look at a yurt while she was at a local drum camp and she fell in love with it. She loved the patterns of the wood, the light through the canvas, the round window, and the blue sky and clouds passing overhead. George initially didn't understand why Lindsey wanted to spend her savings on the yurt. He didn't know what one was, but now he is as enthralled with it as Lindsey is and they often sleep out there with their dog, Ry. "George loves it now," she says, "but it is really my space. It really was worth the investment."

The yurt is 14 feet (4 meters) in diameter. The yurt, or ger as it is also called, originates in Central Asia and was used as a portable dwelling by nomadic people. It may not look big from the outside, but the height and light inside give an impression of lots of space.

above The round window gives a lovely view of the surrounding Suffolk meadows and woods.

opposite and inset Colorful African plastic rugs cover the floor of the yurt and Lindsey's collection of African fabrics are used everywhere, including on the bed and on the chairs and table. With the criss-cross pattern of the yurt's supporting walls and the bunting, there is pattern and color everywhere.

overleaf Lindsey has furnished the yurt with all the essentials for comfortable day-to-day living, including a bed for Ry, her dog.

Lindsey loves homemaking and her surroundings are very important to her. The yurt is beautifully colorful with African plastic rugs, cloths, bunting, tablecloths, bowls of fruit, and flowers from the garden. She spends time in it nearly every day.

If George is away on business, Lindsey and the dog move into the yurt, "practically living there," and she sleeps there, listening to the night sounds of scuttling creatures, swooping owls, the occasional "yell" of a fox or muntjac deer, and the cows moving through the field nearby, munching grass as they pass by. Lindsey can watch the stars through the circular "eye of heaven" at the top of the yurt or listen to the patter of rain. She says, "It is lovely in the rain with the wood burner lit." Lighting is provided by solar lamps and candles.

Another of Lindsey's loves is to play the balafon (a West African xylophone) alone or with friends and the gentle music played on the wood sounds wonderful in the yurt. She has had up to four friends playing and likes that the large balafons can be left in place, ready for another day. Lindsey is a great cook and loves entertaining friends and eating around the table in the yurt or outside.

"The other night when I was playing the balafon, George looked out of the cottage window and saw the cows gathered around the yurt in a semi-circle, listening to the music. He came out to tell me about the audience and the next day it happened again." It appears cows love music.

This is the fifth year the yurt has been up. Last time it was erected in the garden, but this year it has been sited in the field with a temporary fence around it to keep nosy cows at a little distance. Lindsey loves the fact that there is no phone, no internet, and no electricity. Their business has grown and they have become busier and busier, but the yurt is an island away from the "press and stress" of being self-employed. The yurt has been an antidote to work and a lifeline for Lindsey. She can escape to another world with no expectations of her to do anything: "I don't feel guilty about stopping."

Marie and her partner, Mark, live in the Suffolk village of Sweffling where they own a lovely old pub. When they first viewed the property, the pub had been closed for five years and although they do now open for business at weekends, it was the land behind the pub that drew them there.

It is on this land that they now run a busy and very successful eco-campsite with Mongolian-style yurts, Native American-style tipis, traveler's vans, and a beautiful star-gazing hut. The campsite is called Alde Garden.

With this busy life of running the pub and the campsite, Marie felt the need to have a place where she could get away from the business. At the top of the hill she found her spot and local shed-builder Jon began building her hut. Once he had constructed the building, Marie took on the interior.

The approach from the pub is through a stick-built gate which leads to a wonderful conglomeration of tipis, huts, and yurts, as well as a jungle kitchen for the use of the campers, a fire pit with an ornate firegrate made by a friend, and even a long-drop eco loo. All of this is surrounded by a perimeter of trees and hedges. Rustic pathways take you to the various different parts of the site, surprising and delighting as each tucked-away camping opportunity reveals itself.

The gardens are deliberately designed to be wild, with hedges, trees, and shrubs giving each area of the campsite its own space and privacy. Marie and Mark are committed to looking after the environment and doing things as naturally as possible, and describe this as a wildlife garden. There are ducks and chickens running around, and their compost is used for the vegetables and hedges. Marie wanted people to feel as though they had pitched up in the wild countryside.

far right The rustic gate gives access to a path that leads to the eco-camp where guests can stay in a variety of yurts, tipis, and travelers' vans, tucked away behind hedges and trees.

right The "mod-cons" comprise an open communal kitchen and a long-drop compost loo.

below Beyond the fire pit with its ornate fire tripod and up the hill is a view of a yurt, a tipi, and, tucked away, Marie's own retreat.

below right The open kitchen is at the bottom of the hill and has everything needed for self-catering. Guests can take their meals in their accommodation, at the picnic-style table and chairs, or sitting around a fire at night.

left The unusual star-gazing hut on stilts was inspired by an experience in New Zealand. It is completely hidden away among the trees and shrubs.

top The hut just has a bed with a log on each side for candle lamps, but the view of the stars through the glass roof panels is magical.

above The rest of the roof is innovatively tiled with old LPs, which buckle in the heat but keep the hut dry.

This ethos runs to the structure of Marie's own hut. The ash beams in the roof were steam bent by Mark and the paint is lime-based clay with natural terra-cotta tints. The gutter is made from ash. Marie reckons that about 80 percent of the hut is made from recycled materials. The whole structure is built on wheels, which may have come from an old hay cart.

Climbing up the hill you can see the gray of the wood, mellowed by the sun and rain. The hut sits high on its wheels and to get inside there are steep steps made from two logs. Marie has a passion for ledge and brace doors, so Jon found her one from one of his sources. The arched windows were also one of his finds. Inside, the flooring is made from an old school floor. They used most of the wood during the pub renovations, but there was just enough left over for the hut.

"I can retreat up here and no one knows I am here,
but I can still keep an eye on the outside if I want."

left and opposite A friend nicknamed "Metal Mark" made the wood burner from an empty gas cylinder, backing the surround with sheet metal to protect the wood from the heat. Marie enjoyed creating the beautiful, colorful, and cozy interior. The natural colors, the hand-sculpted roof, and clever recycling of found objects contribute to the feeling of a rustic hideaway.

opposite below Marie has made hooks out of suitably shaped pieces of wild wood on the ledge and brace door.

below On the far wall is a curtain rail made from an old hoe, while the benches, which convert into a bed, are made from recycled pallets. The colorful pillows were a gift from a local friend.

The two foldaway beds are made from pallets. The table is a support for a bed, and the tabletop lifts up to reveal a wood store for the wood burner. This was created from an old gas cylinder and the decoration around it was made by their friend "Metal Mark." Next to it is a cupboard which had a previous life as a meat safe.

The stained-glass window was originally in a cottage where it looked incongruous, so they found it a new home and it's perfect at one end of the hut, with a shelf above it made from a plank of elm. A pretty green light filters through glass bricks which reflect the trees behind the hut—the bricks were a find from another friend. Branch hooks and a curtain pole made from an old garden hoe add to the rustic charm of this hand-made hut. Cushions in strong Moroccan colors were kindly made by a woman in the village, and in the spirit of generosity so prevalent in this project, she wouldn't accept any payment for her work.

Although this is Marie's space, she offers it from time to time to friends who have supported them physically and emotionally. She calls it a "gift folly" and won't take payment from those who have been so helpful over the years.

When Marie uses this space for herself, she calls it her hiding place where she can shut the door and no one know she is there, although she can see approaching visitors in the glass reflection of the wood burner. Ultimately, this is what Marie calls her indulgence, her place without clutter, and a place that calms her.

left and opposite As well as the tipis and yurts, guests can stay in this pretty green "gypsy" caravan, which is decorated and trimmed in yellows and creams. Light comes through the glass "mollycroft" on the roof.

opposite below left and right The interior of the caravan is prettily decorated in cream with a raised bed and storage underneath. When the door is flung open, the view is framed by the stable doors which are decorated with lovely pink flowers and scrolls.

Chapter 3

Urban
huts and hideaways

City living often places restrictions on the amount of space available in a traditional home, so ingenious solutions to meet the needs for work, living, and leisure are often found in very small spaces. Garages are converted, existing sheds given makeovers, or exciting and innovative new builds in cob, mud, and timber take shape. Trailer bases are even pressed into use to form the "foundations" for tiny houses.

In this chapter we find a wide variety of urban huts and hideaways, from tiny houses to backyard cottages, from working offices and music and art studios to an Airbnb in a mud hut and a boathouse nowhere near the sea. The space may be restricted, but what happens inside certainly isn't.

Some retreats are traditional—the shed behind the house or at the bottom of the garden—and some are unconventional, squeezing into extraordinary spaces or even capable of moving from place to place. One tiny home is parked up between a friend's house and the garage next door, with only room for a table and chair outside. Some are ethical or economic solutions to the challenges of city living.

Women's sheds have become very visible in recent years and women are seeing the possibilities at the end of the garden or backyard or in the previously wild and unkempt areas they see as they look out of their windows. What comes through for many is the need for women's own spaces to work or play. This chapter is a journey down some of the paths we find in our cities and towns.

This apparent woodland setting would make you think that **Karin** lives in a rural area rather than as part of a "tiny house" community, located behind an ordinary urban house. The street is, admittedly, a leafy street, but it is still in the bustling city of Portland.

"Tiny houses" are built on trailer bases and are therefore dependent on finding somewhere to park them. The owner of this house is part of the community, and has allowed four tiny homes to settle in the backyard. Here, the residents live in close proximity, growing their vegetables. They have come up with just six miraculous rules for living together, one of which is not to annoy each other; another is not to leave junk on view. The four remaining rules cover committing to a few hours of communal work and involvement in various projects. Together they have built a wonderful community, with the bonus of fabulous neighbors so they don't have to move again.

Karin has taken quite a personal journey to arrive at this small "tiny house" community. She spent six years studying Chinese medicine—"sitting on my bottom and not using my body." When she graduated, she wanted a radical shift in her life. She knew nothing about building and was stimulated to learn a new skill. So began the story of her tiny house.

opposite and right Karin had to move her tiny home a few times before she found this small "tiny house" community where she has settled her blue and yellow little house next to a much-loved plum tree.

"As soon as I came across tiny homes, I knew that this was what I wanted ... This is the way I want to live and it is the best thing I have ever done."

She found a space in a friend's backyard and bought a trailer base. There she built her new home, but the neighbors complained about the presence of the tiny house and she had to move on. The laws regarding the siting of tiny houses seem to vary from one district to another and these dwellings seem, at the moment, to be a gray area legally. Karin describes it as "allegal." Being on wheels allows these popular living solutions to circumvent normal regulations, but some rules pertaining to, say, recreation vehicles (RVs) can apply, so in order to keep these homes on the right side of the law, many are described as spare bedrooms or annexes. Karin comments that in a world where some people are finding their own solutions to housing and new ways of living, support from more local authorities would be welcome.

Karin's mother's husband lent her the tools for her build. At the start, she didn't know one type of saw from another, but she's come a long way since then. She had plans, but let the build evolve slowly as she didn't want to make mistakes. The tiny house is "stick built" or timber-framed. It is partly clad with board-and-batten timber and plywood paneling. Friends helped out and it took three months to reach the weatherproof stage. It was from then that Karin could take her time "pottering about ... thinking and enjoying letting the interior evolve." She first painted it a rich buttery yellow—a color that took a little getting used to. Then she decided to paint it periwinkle blue and so, at the time we visited, it was both yellow and blue, trimmed with white to frame the bright colors.

After moving her home a few times, Karin met Lina Menard and moved to their small developing community. She says, "It was perfect—the best

above The ladder up to the sleeping platform also acts as storage space.

opposite above Karin's love of color, influenced by her heritage and travels, is reflected in her use of bright reds, colorful fabrics, and her collection of Turkish rugs.

opposite below A compact kitchen and bathroom use clever design and storage solutions to make the interior work well.

thing I have ever done." She found her spot next to a plum tree, which has provided an abundance of fruit over the years. "It is," she says, "my closest friend."

Karin firmly states that this is the way she wants to live. Buying a traditional house would have involved mortgages and debt, which is not for her. Karin thinks she has spent about $20,000 in all. The money that would have been spent on a mortgage paid not only for her home, but also enabled her to set up her Chinese medicine clinic.

Karin is also a celebrant and her ex-husband, Roger Parramore, who is internationally known as a glass artist, has made her the most beautiful set of glass vessels to use in wedding rituals. They are on display on a high shelf to keep them safe. Karin is interested in many spiritual traditions, including Sufism.

She says that her house has a Central Asian theme, partly due to her interests but also her heritage. She has bought many carpets back from Turkey and the colors she has used in decorating reflect the yarns used in these carpets, with green, blue, orange, red, and pink seen on the walls and in the fabrics she has used. During dismal winters the colors keep her alive.

The tiny house feels spacious and, as with all tiny houses, the storage systems really matter. The wooden steps up to the sleeping loft also act as shelves and at one end of the house is a concealed storage area. Karin has never been one to accumulate possessions, and follows the adage, "Objects need to be beautiful or useful ... and bring you joy."

Karin says that there are fewer than fifty women with tiny homes of their own. She is proud to be a woman in her tiny house community in independently minded Portland.

Alex's garden—an urban oasis of patio, lawn, and pots in Acton, west London—is hidden behind her large house and framed by mature trees. Down a paved path and past a mini garden shed is her upholstery shed. This is a functional working shed, constructed by Suffolk-based shed-builder Jon, who was also employed by her friend Celeste not many streets away (see page 120).

This shed needed to be light, hence the large, steel-framed Crittall windows that pivot horizontally to open. These were a fortunate find by Jon. Word of mouth has led to many of his sheds finding their own individual style as Jon follows their owners' dreams and aspirations and uses his building and recycling skills to deliver something special for his clients (see page 78 for the Suffolk retreat he built for Marie).

Although Alex doesn't primarily make a living from her upholstery, she does work to commission and also teaches other women how to upholster. They bring their own furniture finds and learn how to revamp them into something wonderful that they can be proud of. This is a space to work and a space to share, to create new bespoke furniture.

The shed has equipment everywhere, and a chair sits on the bench waiting to be transformed with Alex's expertise. Tools line one wall and rolls of fabric lean against another. Tins and boxes of trimmings abound. There are two sewing machines, one of which is an industrial model for the heavy-duty work. When the sewing machines are not whirring away, the only sounds are the birds and the subdued noise of trains running along the railway line, the clickety-clack muffled by the trees.

Alex uses the shed all year round, so it is well insulated and heated. The interior is plain and light, with a functional pale wooden floor. It is the fabrics and trimmings which add a mass of color, brought to life by the shafts of light coming through the windows and the roof light. Practical strip lighting allows Alex to work at night or in winter, when good daylight

above Alex has a layered garden in front of her shed, with planters of herbs, pots of flowers and ornamental grasses, and even a couple of potato bags.

opposite above and below The shed is framed on three sides by mature trees. The huge Crittall windows let in plenty of light for Alex as she works on bringing life to old chairs through her upholstery skills.

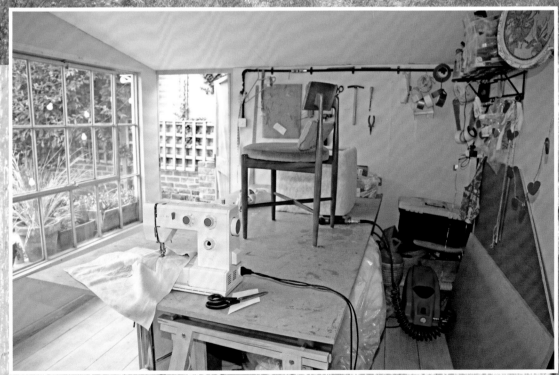

is scarce. There is little embellishment. apart from a decorative parasol, a brightly colored bird, and some heart-shaped lights. The fabrics, the shape of the chairs, and the trimmings are all she needs to inspire her.

Outside the shed are many pots and planters, some of them sitting on old logs to give them height, with the different levels adding interest. Here there are flowers, grasses, salad plants, and even potatoes growing in sacks. The walls of the shed are weatherboarded and painted a pale blue-gray. Above the windows is a fake porthole—an amusing find which makes Alex smile. Solar lights are strung across the front, making the shed a pretty sight at night.

At the rear of the house, the large kitchen has glass fold-back doors, spanning the width of the room and looking out onto the garden, the shed, and the trees, making a peaceful view while the city goes about its business all around.

above left The swivelled Crittall windows create an unusual sculptural effect when open.

above When Alex works by the window, enjoying the light, she can look back up the garden to the house.

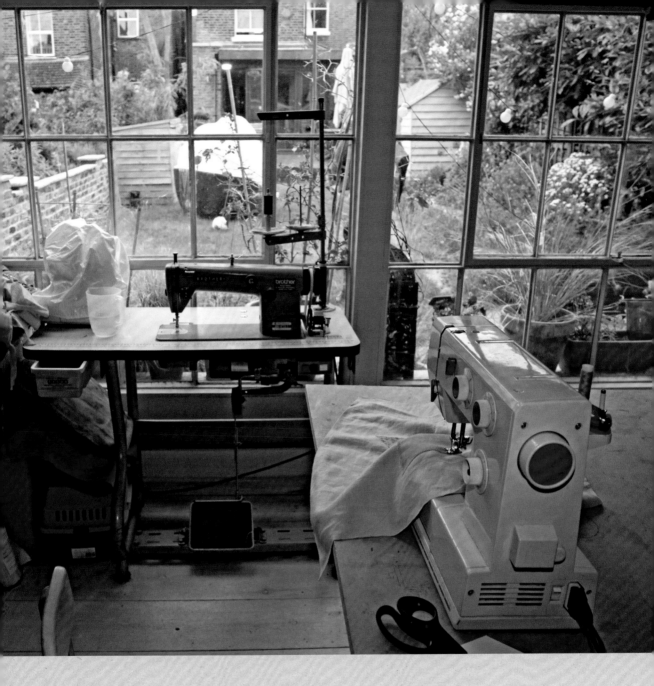

"The shed looks like it's been there for a while ... the cat likes to sunbathe on the roof and a fox has been spotted walking across the slate tiles."

above Michelle's tiny house is clad with cedar tongue and groove and corrugated metal.

opposite Although the tiny house is not quite finished, the basic structure is there. Michelle already has the 1950s kitchen ready to install as part of her love for "modern nostalgia."

overleaf When Michelle has finished building her tiny home, she hopes to find a farm or winery where she can live and work.

Michelle's tiny house is to be found in Sherwood, to the south of the city of Portland, Oregon. Michelle has had many setbacks in life, and the tiny house is her venture into creating a home for herself that no one can take away. She had gone through a challenging childhood being fostered by her grandparents, before leaving at eighteen to get married. Sadly this didn't work out. After more false starts and sadness, she decided to take her destiny into her own hands and moved to Oregon with her two children, two cats, and two dogs. It was here that she found her feet, used her resilience and resourcefulness, and took charge of her life.

The tiny house is, for her, all about being herself, being safe—emotionally and financially—having somewhere to socialize, and, most of all, giving her a sense of home.

Michelle's tiny dwelling sits in front of a small wooden house where she has been living for some time. It sits on a 24-foot flat-bed trailer base, bought at a knock-down price as it had a bit of damage, which has now been repaired. She says, "When the children leave home, this will be my downsize." This doesn't feel as though it will be too much of a sacrifice as there are two sleeping lofts and the height and size give her enough space not to feel cramped. The lounge is a good size and the chairs she designed have a lift-up front to allow for storage. The stairs are made of high-quality plywood, with the end grains being part of the design. Shoe drawers are incorporated into the first two steps.

Michelle has a very innovative approach toward funding her home, and has managed to gain sponsorship for the majority of the build and fittings. This is because many businesses have woken up to the fact that the Tiny House movement is a potentially lucrative market. In return, Michelle blogs, uses social media, and gives talks to promote her build and publicize the companies who have contributed to the house. On this basis, insulation, materials, fabrics, lighting, and much more have been supplied. She has approached over twenty sponsors and $17,000 worth of goods and services have gone into the build. Her favorite price is "next-to-nothing"!

Not all the materials are new. The interior walls in Michelle's sleeping loft
are recycled cladding rescued from a dilapidated 1890s beach hut. Michelle
believes in a mixture of what she calls "modern nostalgia," which means
that everything works with a touch of the old and recycled for character.
The ladder to the second loft is a lucky find. Originally covered in paint and
grime, she had it sand blasted to get rid of rust and corrosion, then powder-
coated using a metallic process, but the aged patina remains. When not in
use, she will hang it on the wall in the lounge area "as a piece of art."

Michelle considered installing solar power but believes it is not yet
sufficiently economic, so instead she uses energy-efficient LED lighting
throughout. The home isn't finished yet but completion isn't far off. The
bathroom and a 1950s kitchen remain to be installed. Michelle loves to cook
so the kitchen is important to her.

When it's finished, she will be looking for a place in the countryside
where she can tow her home and settle. She really would like to work on a
horse farm or other animal-focused farm and live there in return for work
and marketing. She says that she will have very little impact on the land or

her hosts, as all she needs is an electric extension cable and a garden hose. A composting loo will complete her low-impact lifestyle.

Michelle, like other tiny homers, is very aware of the legality issues surrounding tiny houses on wheels. In her region of Oregon there are generous zoning requirements, but she says, "If I moved four miles in a different direction, they would be a lot stricter." For now, she is looking forward to full autonomy and the adventures having the tiny house will bring. There is already a sense of being on the move with her collection of licence plates sent to her from all over the USA.

Michelle is also aware that being "cute" is an attractive prospect for future hosts to think about when she is looking for a place to settle. To this end, the outside is a mixture of vertical cedar tongue and groove and corrugated metal. It is an attractive, contemporary look that should please others—and certainly pleases Michelle.

She also has "Betsy"—a tiny 1950s caravan, which is a traveling home when she feels the urge to get away. This is the predecessor to the tiny build, and furnishing it gave Michelle the confidence to take on the much more ambitious construction project. Her boyfriend says it is a place she goes to when she is mad at him. She quips, "He lives two hundred miles away!"

Michelle believes, "You don't have to have all the answers, but what's next only ... learning as you go along"—a sentiment that applies as much to life as to this build.

below Michelle is a glamping enthusiast and "Betsy" is her little vintage caravan, which she uses to get away and meet other enthusiasts. This was her first foray into compact furnishing.

"When I move, I want to move to the **countryside** and live on a horse farm or maybe a winery. I would like to park **under a cedar tree.**"

"It isn't usually this tidy. When we are working there are lyric sheets all over the floor."

Ellie is a composer, songwriter, string arranger, and performer. She collaborates with many different people on various styles of music, from TV adverts to pop songs, music libraries, and children's music.

When she and her family were looking for a new home in Brighton, on England's south coast, she attached one very important condition: she needed to have her own recording studio, and this couldn't get lost in the list of other family priorities. "When we viewed the house with its falling down, disused garage, I just knew this place would be perfect!"

The rustic blue-painted exterior—its striking mural was painted by her artist friend Fay Chadburn—now hides a very contemporary studio.

Inside, the studio is both functional and beautifully decorated, allowing Ellie and her collaborators to work and relax in comfort. The walls of the main studio are painted a rich red, while the carpet and sofa are a soft cream. There is underfloor heating and insulation. A necessity was that it be soundproofed to protect the neighbors. There is a second area used for storage. A desk with computers allows her to record strings and vocals using specialist computer programs.

On the day of our visit, Ellie explains, "It isn't usually this tidy—when we are working, there are lyric sheets all over the floor, and empty tea cups and instruments everywhere!"

above Ellie's recording desk faces on to the garden and is where the mixing and magic come together.

right In a corner on a table are just some of Ellie's large collection of musical instruments, including an "add a random noise" basket.

above Ellie's recording desk faces on to the garden and is where the mixing and magic come together.

right In a corner on a table are just some of Ellie's large collection of musical instruments, including an "add a random noise" basket.

Jos's studio sits in the small but pretty garden behind her home in a row of typically English houses in the city of Norwich. The garden is brick paved with lots of pot plants, flower beds, and hanging baskets, and has the feel of a courtyard. Although in the city, when Jos is gardening or sitting at the small round table, it feels secluded and private.

Jos found a carpenter/joiner to make the studio to her own specification and to fit her small garden. It soon became her own private space and her painting studio. For Jos, it is important not to work in the house—she prefers to keep the two spaces separate and defined.

Like most painters, Jos values the light. The walls are white and plenty of natural light comes through windows on one side of the studio, the glass-paned door, and the roof, which is made from transparent corrugated plastic.

Although her small paintings line the walls and sit on worksurfaces, and the shelves hold an array of canvases, and materials, there is a feeling of order and calm. There is also lots of storage in a semi-loft area to keep canvases and so on out of the way. Jos says if she could build the studio again, it would be more modern but it works as it is.

Jos's profession was as an art therapist, working in the field of mental health. It was when she was made redundant that her focus could change, and her work became more meditative and balanced. She says of painting, "It keeps me sane." Her paintings are mainly still lives including juxtapositions of objects that have some meaning for Jos. It isn't always immediately clear to the viewer how the object relates to the painting and this makes her work very intriguing. In one painting, for example, she has included an Italian cup her father brought back from Perugia, north of Rome. She explains that he died when she was young and this could be seen as a small homage to him.

Jos exhibits and sells her work regularly, including through the Fairhurst Gallery in Norwich. She usually exhibits twice a month and takes part every other year in the Norfolk Open Studios event. Art lovers can come down an alley to find this hidden studio and her intriguing paintings on display. She paints every day if she isn't doing anything else, and finds the mornings are the best time for her. Each painting takes about five or six days to complete.

opposite Jos has her small eclectic paintings which include disparate yet related scenes and objects, on show around her studio.

opposite below The deceptively spacious studio was built to fit into the space at the bottom of her compact city garden.

Julia is a painter and artist, a dowser, and a specialist in flower remedies, based in Gloucestershire, in the west of England. She has found that having her own space to think, paint, meditate, and watch nature has become more important than ever since her life became more challenging. Her husband has his own shed on one side of the garden, and she has hers.

Her shed is on the site of an old one which had rotted away. While she was wondering if she could save up for a new one, a grateful client explained that she had intended to leave Julia some money in her will but then said, "I would like to give it to you now." This generous act of gratitude enabled Julia to have her shed.

And so, halfway up the garden, she has her own space where she sits watching both her inner and outer landscapes and the wildlife.

Julia and her husband bought this house, larger than their previous home, when Julia's mother died. The large garden, on a steep Stroud hill, is very important to Julia. She has planted it with flowers for bees and other pollinating insects, and created a semi-wild area at the top of the hill. Paths wind through the shrubs and wild areas, leading to a seat at the very top of the garden.

opposite This small shed contains everything Julia needs to garden, paint, meditate, or watch the wildlife visiting the garden.

below Julia has a view of her husband's shed, which sits on the other side of the garden.

"I plant for pleasure and for wildlife."

On display inside the shed is an enigmatic painting of a woman with two shafts of light balancing on her hands. "Something about balance ..." Julia offers. On the wall there is a shamanic figure she has made from wood and feathers. On days when the weather is good, she can sit outside on the patio unless, of course, she is gardening.

On the wide slatted shelf facing down the garden toward the house are plants and a few special objects, and next to the door, in a neat row, are her gardening tools. Below the shelf are drawers for seeds and small hand tools. This is a multifunctional shed, yet kept simple and uncluttered. It meets Julia's needs. She can sit on the camping chair and reach for her binoculars to bird watch and see if any animals, such as badgers or foxes, might wander into this welcoming refuge.

This is a shed without pretensions to be anything else but a shed. The walls are left undecorated inside and out and yet it is so much more than a shed. It is a hide and a refuge; a place to be and to meditate; to create and paint, and to venture out into her beautiful hillside garden to plant for pleasure and for wildlife.

above Pretty containers hold dried treasures from the garden and a succulent, like tiny sculptures from nature.

opposite Julia's shed is to be found halfway up the semi-wild garden, which is a hillside oasis for birds, bees, and other urban wildlife.

left On the veranda there is just enough room for a table, a chair, and a statue of Buddha.

opposite The sitting room is a wonderful mixture of exotic fabrics, drapes, and cushions, and the base of the sofa doubles up as a mattress for guests.

opposite inset The miniature Tanpura, a Moroccan star lamp, and another Buddha have one of the three recycled screen panels as a backdrop.

"When I got rid of stuff, I kept my best decorative pieces."

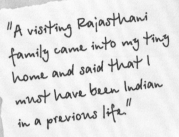

right Anita's bedroom has pale green fabrics which, together with daylight from the skylight and window, help to maximize the feeling of space. The water collection tank nestles at the end of her bed.

"A visiting Rajasthani family came into my tiny home and said that I must have been Indian in a previous life."

When Anita divested herself of her belongings before moving into the tiny home, she kept just the decorative pieces she loved. One of the paths Anita follows is that of Buddhism, and her Buddha from Thailand is a treasured possession. There are Moroccan lamps everywhere. A miniature stringed musical instrument, the Tanpura, is there just for show—this long-necked Indian instrument is played as an accompanying drone in many forms of Indian music. A Rajasthani family who visited commented that it was as though she had had a previous life in that part of India.

There is no sign of scrimping in Anita's decor, which includes rich fabrics from India, Morocco, and Bali. She has heating from her solar panels, and touches of luxury, such as the tiles on the bathroom floor. Although Anita thought they were pricey, the area to be tiled was so small she felt she could justify it. She has a proper tiny tub from an RV (recreational vehicle) with a white tiling surround.

Anita loves copper with its beautiful metallic pink. She had wanted a copper roof but this metal is too soft for a home that might be on the move, so she had the roof painted with copper paint instead. She has a beaten copper sink, which was the first thing she bought when planning her home. Below the wood burner is a counter top also made of copper. "It's high maintenance," she says "but worth it."

Anita used to work as a computer clerk, but her love of animals and nature has led her to retrain as a pet massage practitioner and aromatherapist. She is also a Reiki master and gardener. She has dreams of running an animal sanctuary before too long and she has a view to the future. Everything has been done to save energy and resources—she has reduced her running costs by 70 percent. There is rainwater collection from the roof and the tank sits at the bottom of her bed. She uses LED lighting. As her plan is to be able to live off-grid, Anita wants to become 100 percent solar-powered so that she can be self-reliant wherever she is, but at the moment she is still on mains electricity. To fulfill her dreams and move her home, she will need a tow but she is understandably anxious about relocating something 13½ feet (4m) high. Anita tells me, "It is scary to move them."

All Anita's choices lead to a truer and simpler life. She follows Gandhi's philosophy that "in a gentle way you can shape the world … for the benefit of all beings." She describes herself as "a mindful rebel."

above The sitting room is luxurious, with strong influences from North Africa and India. The carved screen and drapes add to the exotic feel of this room with its half-arched ceiling.

"Knowing that the studio was being built helped me cope with all the late nights trying to meet deadlines."

Go through a terraced family house on one of the many steep hills in Stroud and into the garden, down some steep steps and past a wooden playhouse and a shed, and there you will find **Martha**'s studio.

Martha is a children's book illustrator and artist. In her studio at the end of her Gloucestershire garden she illustrates books, listen to records, writes, and doodles. She also runs workshops for children, explaining that "it's a welcome change from working alone and one that always reminds me how much fun creative work can be, especially with children."

Before her purpose-built studio arrived, Martha used to work on a coffee table or on a table in her bedroom. She also had a baby. She says, "I painted in the evenings and while my one-year-old had her daytime naps, and her naps never seemed long enough for the work that I wanted to do … and I had to clear it all up whenever I stopped."

As the illustrator of several successful books, including *One Lucky Duck* by Alison Maloney and *Quiet as a Mouse*, there came a point when Martha had earned enough to afford her own space. She found an excellent builder and watched with wonder as her shed took shape.

previous pages At the end of a long garden is the studio Martha had built.

above and above right Martha has space for her own work and for workshops. Examples of her art and illustrations sit on her easel.

"One day, when the walls and roof had gone up, I walked in with my toddler and the song 'Young at Heart' by The Bluebells was playing on the radio. I danced around with her in my arms and for the first time I had a glimpse of how wonderful it would be. Knowing that it was being built helped me cope with all the late nights trying to meet deadlines."

The design is simple and functional, with lots of light streaming in through the windows, doors, and roof lights. Painted white, the walls provide a backdrop to all the wonderful drawings and paintings Martha is working on, and children's art hangs everywhere. The work is about and by children, giving her studio freshness and joy.

Although fully insulated, there is a wood burner for chilly days, and a sofa with throws adds to the potential for coziness in this otherwise working studio. As well as the brushes and paints, there is a butler's sink with an old mirror behind it. The large easel is a prized possession which Martha acquired when living in London—someone was throwing it away and she's been "lugging it about" ever since. There are shelves for books, a table to work at, and plenty of floor to spread out on.

Martha says, "It's a place where I can leave the chaos of a busy family life behind and just focus on making things. It's more than just a building where I work—it's a place where I can breathe more slowly and give myself time to think things through without interruption; where I can remind myself to experiment and play around with new ideas; and where I can feel like myself again when life is busy in other ways. When I know I have a whole day in the studio coming up, I feel very happy and am probably a calmer parent." Most weekdays Martha goes straight to the studio after the school run. If a deadline is looming, she accepts that the house becomes more disordered than usual.

"I often write for a bit when I first get in, which can help to clear my head, and then start drawing or painting. Sometimes if I get a bit stuck on a project, I remind myself to do something playful, such as collage, where I'm not worried about the outcome. Some of my favorite ideas have come out of these moments. I've had the studio for three years, and still feel very, very lucky to have it."

above Martha has
created an eclectic mix
of the practical and the
beautiful. An ornate
mirror stands behind
the sink and the wood
burner keeps the studio
useable all year round.

left Pots and tins hold
brushes, pens, and
whatever else Martha
needs to create her
lovely book illustrations.

above Rosa has made the interior of the shed into a wonderful and colorful testament to her creative and inner life.

opposite It is only when the double doors of this unprepossessing green shed open that the magic of the interior is revealed.

Rosa's shed is in the back garden of her Gloucestershire house and is reached along a paved path. The dark green shed looks ordinary enough at first sight, but is full of surprise and delight.

When Rosa opens the door, the first thing you see is a near full-sized figure sitting against the wall. She has a soft, gentle face and is dressed in the most sumptuous clothes in shades of purple. She has an embroidered hat, purple and lilac socks, and rainbow fingerless gloves. She is part of Rosa's art life and an expression of herself and her life so far.

This "young lady," created by Rosa, sits in a beautiful chair found in Ruskin Mill, near Stroud. Rosa crafted a papier mâché face and hands, while the rest of the body is stuffed with old clothes. Prior to moving the figure into the hut, Rosa sat her in the back of her car! Now she is guardian of the shed.

Rosa has also made another smaller female figure in similar colors, an older version of herself, who sits in the crook of the younger lady's arm. Healing crystals have been placed there to help the "younger me look after the older me."

Polly has a boathouse nowhere near the sea. Instead, it is in a quiet backyard in Portland, Oregon.

She named her hideaway "The Boathouse" to honor the many summers she spent on the coast of Maine, on the San Juan Islands of Puget Sound, and on various rivers and lakes where she has kayaked, paddled, rowed, and sailed a variety of small craft. Her childhood memories are based on the east coast. She says, "The Atlantic is different. The flora and fauna are different. The sea smells brinier and the forests more fragrant."

Of The Boathouse, Polly says, "In short, it is the place I wish I could have on any waterway, but alas, I am land locked." Nevertheless, she wanted it to evoke her childhood in Maine and time spent with her grandmother who, she remembers, had an ocean pool. The sweet smell of cedar cladding triggers some of those memories. Family has continued to be important in her life and she built The Boathouse so that her parents could visit. Her children used it for sleepovers and they loved having friends to stay. Over the years The Boathouse has changed in tandem with life's transitions.

opposite Polly has collected lobster floats over the years to decorate her inland boathouse, reminding her of great times spent with family and on ocean vacations.

right The Boathouse is decorated and dressed with fresh blues, as well as photos and paintings of water scenes.

above There are eating and relaxing areas on the decked patio and behind the blue screens, which afford guests some privacy from the main house.

There is a touch of the theatrical about The Boathouse. Polly's inventiveness comes from her background as a stage designer and her love of designing environments for theater, opera, film, animation, and landscape. In her imagination there might be a firetower attached to the building—"but that might upset the neighbors!"—or a horse trailer, or ... "If I could just work on interesting projects like my boathouse, or take properties that would otherwise be considered too tasteless for some people's sensibilities and transform them, I would be a very happy designer, indeed."

The exterior wood cladding on The Boathouse has been left unpainted and a collection of lobster floats decorate one wall. An oar above the door continues the seafaring theme.

Inside, The Boathouse is bright and light and equipped with a double bed, small writing table, and cupboards for stashing gear and a hammock. The room has electricity and wi-fi, but no plumbing. It is heated by a space heater in the winter, meaning it is comfortable for guests all year round. The interior walls are painted light blue and the coastal theme continues with driftwood holding the windows open, and more oars. The shelves hold beachcombing finds—fossils, stones, and sea urchins—and hanging on the walls there are photos of the seashore and a watercolor painting by Wini Smart, who was a well-known artist when Polly was young. The painting, she says, "is a real touchstone for me."

The textured treatments on the glass panes of the door come from a theater backdrop Polly made for the opera "Carmen." Metallic paint was used on muslin and the fabric has now found a new use here.

Outside The Boathouse is a "sitting room" hidden by cornflower blue painted screens set on pale lilac decking. It has an outside oven and seats made from pallets with vintage print pillows. Fairy lights provide the night-time sparkle. The quirky outdoor shower was converted from the children's fort that they had long outgrown. "They wouldn't let me take it down to build the outdoor shower I wanted, so my (then) husband and I agreed to create the shower up in the fort, installing stairs and enclosing the space with cedar fence boards and salvaged windows from an old Victorian house." The roof is made of clear corrugated plastic. The windows are random in size, painted blue, and one is mirrored. There are bird houses, made by Polly, all around the top of the shower, giving a strange castellation to the exterior. A fort-like feeling still exists as visitors need to climb up to the shower on steep steps. Ledges for soap, hooks, and a mirror equip the space.

Polly says that building The Boathouse has helped her through illness and adversity and "it has been a lovely thing." A friend has her eye on it, commenting that she knows it is there if she ever wants to run away!

Polly is willing to share this special place and now runs it as a B&B, with guests using the cooking and bathroom facilities in the main house. Sometimes she blocks out time and leaves The Boathouse free so that she can have it to herself as a refuge from a busy life and a household full of young people. In the winter, Polly confides, it is the perfect place to "hole up with a coffee or a scotch."

below The outdoor shower is an ingenious and fun transformation of the children's old fort. It has a corrugated plastic roof and recycled windows, one of which is usefully mirrored on the inside.

Susanna lives in a cob house in the backyard of her house in Portland, Oregon. She originally rented the home and loved both the house and the leafy neighborhood so much that she bought the property when the opportunity arose. She inherited some money from her beloved grandmother and, at the same time, the house was put up for sale. Susanna says, "It felt as though the stars were aligned."

Susanna had done some building with others and wanted to construct a cob house for herself. This property had sufficient space in its backyard, so she built the cob house in 2011 and has lived in it ever since. What she loved about the build was that the collaboration involved all sorts of people, including visionary artists. She says that the building process felt personal and was a wonderful journey for her and for her vision of future art and building.

Susanna calls her naturally built cob house "The Love Shack" or "The Hobbit Hole." The walls are cob, with the exterior painted a soft warm lilac and a sculpted seat painted brown. At the end of the seat and under the wide porch is a pizza oven shaped into a snail, forming part of the outside kitchen. The kitchen has lots of wooden cabinets and shelves to provide storage, and pots hang from the porch roof. The porch over the seating area is tiled with recycled ducting. "Cutting the pieces took the patience of a saint," she recalls.

The walls inside are a beautiful pink. One wall is decorated with a light sculpture made from bottles framed in an irregular white rectangle. Wooden benches and a chest of drawers line the walls, while the bed is draped with a wonderful array of fabrics. These are also used to cover the windows at night and to keep the cob house cool on really hot days. The walls have good thermal qualities, but there are some times when extra heat is needed so Susanna has a

above Behind the cob house is the well-equipped kitchen area with a "snail" pizza oven and, next to that, a sculpted seat under the eaves of the roof.

"There are lots of phases to our projects.
This one has been a wonderful journey."

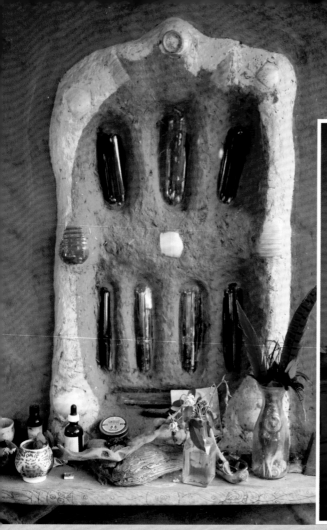

left and opposite Daylight shines through the multi-colored glass bottles inset into a sculpted arch, while shafts of light enter the house through the round windows, which appear to be placed randomly in the cob walls.

opposite below Pans and assorted kitchenware hang from beams in the outdoor kitchen, protected by the roof made from recycled and shaped ducting.

below A collection of Susanna's boots, stacked on a wooden bench outside the house.

overleaf This treehouse was meant to be.

robust-looking, barrel-shaped wood burner for the chilliest days and nights.

The main house is being transformed into a more communal building. Susanna can feel free to be as creative as she wants on her land, and to this end has created an amazing sculptural treehouse high in the curved branches of a mature tree. It turns out that she wasn't the only person who envisioned a treehouse in this corner spot. Many others saw the possibilities and a vision from the past was revealed when a ninety-year-old woman shared her delight at seeing the treehouse. When she was young and living in the neighborhood, she really wanted one but her father wouldn't allow it. It was a marvel to her to see this one nestled among the greenery of the tree. Susanna believes that the treehouse "wanted to be there!"

To help with the treehouse construction, Susanna joined forces with a wonderful builder named SunRay Kelley, a friend of Lloyd Kahn, who has written many books on natural building and tiny homes. Deeply involved in natural building, Susanna thinks he is a genius builder. The design is based on a huge platform with a curved roof soaring above. The sinuous branches are part of the sculptured structure and are not dominated by the almost free-floating roof. It's a place to be or to play or sleep. A welcoming mattress awaits the next brave ladder-climber who wants to gaze at the stars, and Susanna would love to hang canvas pods from the tree to sleep in. "There are lots of phases to our projects! This has been a wonderful journey."

Chapter 4
Hidden
huts and hideaways

For a shed, cabin, or hut to be truly hidden, it has to be apart and out of view of the outside world. There is a need and a desire to move from the busy world to tranquility, especially in the city where the cars, the people, the intensity, and the noise can become too much. Some may love city life, but even they look for an occasional respite to modern living, for green spaces, walks on the heath or the beach, and it is this desire for refuge from chaos that attracts us to hidden places.

When we go to that place of retreat, there is space for us to slow down and process the complexities of living, to be inspired and find ourselves—creatively, maybe spiritually. If we don't want friends or family to interrupt our work or creativity, the door will be shut and the boundaries set so we can have time and space for ourselves.

In this chapter we meet two women who found an amazing field near the sea, completely hidden by mature hedges and trees. In another hideaway, rough sheds nestle near a heath and hold dear memories for a family; a shed on a smallholding provides a retreat; outside a shed on a community garden is an eating area hidden by a grapevine; and a shed-to-be faces on to a wilderness hidden in an old quarry. An old bus provides a sanctuary for a festival organizer when she wants to get away from thousands of festival goers on her land, and a mother and daughter take off for adventures across the USA in an ice-cream van.

One day **Feddy**, who is from Uganda, was walking along a path in London when she saw some allotment gardens located on community land. She was amazed that it was possible to grow food in London—until then she had only grown a few vegetables, such as tomatoes and peppers, on her balcony. So Feddy asked her local council for an allotment. They sent her directions so she could visit her local plot but, being dyslexic, she went to the wrong place. For her, it turned out to be the right place. She was given a plot there, next to the River Lee, and started her garden.

A friend of her partner, Gill, whom she met in Nicaragua, helped her build the shed from found and recycled materials. It is a wonderful mix of double-glazed windows salvaged from a dumpster, timber, and felt cladding. The door, with the house number 55, came from her old home, but apart from this, dumpster-diving provided everything. The graffitied chairs and table came from past lives; the desk from squatting days.

The eating area is hidden from view by a grapevine trellis and has a table covered with a beautiful African cloth. This is where Feddy and Gill can make tea or coffee and relax away from the eyes of the city. "This is my hideout," Feddy says. "I sit, look, and meditate, hidden by the grapevine." On sunny Sundays and fine evenings they have barbecues, and have even managed to eat here in the winter and in the rain.

This garden is an important place of healing for Feddy, so here she is in her element. There are very few people around during the week and having the river next door and a reservoir nearby add to the feeling of an oasis in the city.

above Feddy's recycled shed is hidden by a vigorous grapevine.

opposite Inside the shed there are saved seeds drying in decorative baskets and the pickings of the day.

Feddy goes back to Uganda every year to visit family, keeping her links with her Ugandan heritage strong. She is a great seed-saver and cultivates what African crops she can in London, such as cape gooseberries, banana trees, Ugandan beans, amaranth, and lemongrass. Surpluses mean that she can supply some African shops. Her peas are sprouted from her mother's seeds, and she also grows pumpkins, squash, sweet potatoes, and much more.

Feddy's travels around other parts of the world are also reflected in her vegetable growing, such as the crops of Turkish zucchini and Italian romanesco broccoli. She has planted a strawberry tree, which her mother said would not mature in Feddy's lifetime but it has and now produces wonderful white flowers followed by bright red fruit.

When Feddy took over this plot, there was already an old toolshed there, complete with a pick and shovel that she thinks may have been left there during the Second World War when these gardens were started. She has a panga and jembe, which are traditional African gardening tools. This shed also serves as kitchen and seed store, with shelves of seeds in jars. The shed has storage for plenty of plates and mugs for themselves and for visiting friends. A Portuguese basket and a Ugandan basket sit below the window on another bright African cloth.

There is also a productive greenhouse on the plot, where passionfruit are grown and where trays of onions and garlic are laid out to dry. At harvest time, Feddy offers garlic or some other gift to the figure of a woman on the window ledge in the shed. It is a whimsy of Feddy's.

Feddy says, "I feel at peace here. I have a clock but it's not set as I don't want to know the time. When it gets dark, it is time to go home." Even when she was working full-time, she came here to sit and unwind, "and get my brain back."

left Everything here is gifted or found. There are plenty of plates and cups for outside eating and a clock, which Feddy never looks at. When the daylight fades, it is time to pack up and set off for home.

below left Red and white onions, ready to be preserved until the next crop arrives.

below The grapevines on the pergola provide shade and privacy for Feddy and Gill to sit, contemplate, drink fresh herbal teas, and eat al fresco.

Amanda is a young woman with enterprise. When she was twenty-one, she founded the South Store Cafe in Hillsboro, Oregon. Running a restaurant for ten years gave her the confidence she needed for her next adventure.

Two years ago she decided to travel from the west coast of the USA to the east. She had dreamt of the journey for ten years and when daughter Amelia was eight, she decided that it was time. So she bought an old 1980s ice-cream van she called "Lucy" (or "Lucy Goosy"), planning to sell ice cream along the way so that she and her daughter had an income.

The van is a very reliable box van and rarely breaks down (although there was that time in Oklahoma ...). The interior is quite plain and fitted with freezers for the ice cream. There is a wooden window, which Amanda installed, through which they sell the ice cream. The outside of the van has had a constellation of stars painted onto it and each star is dedicated to remarkable people who have helped her along the way. She says, "There are still some people I owe stars."

Amanda is a musician and singer and planned to travel from festival to festival, so she had a stage built on top of the van for her performances. She plotted their route with stops along the way, often camping off road and away from towns and people. From their home south of Portland city, they set off in spring and toured until the end of the fall. As well as participating in the festivals, they camped a lot and Amanda says, "You really see what's happening at the grass-roots level." By selling ice cream as she went, she met every kind of person.

They found pretty spots to camp in, tucked away where they could relax and feel safe. However, they also stopped at camps that are semi-legal solutions for the thousands who have lost their homes, where people live in tents, RVs, and "shanty" buildings. Amanda found that there are new ways of building communities born out of desperation. People create community initiatives, such as home schools, which she found very inspiring.

On the whole, the experience was fantastic and people were welcoming—Texas was the friendliest state. Any journey on this scale will have its ups and downs—in one town they had four unfortunate experiences in twenty-four hours, but Amelia wrote a witty song about it and the good and the bad balanced out. At one stop they were treated with great suspicion until they found out that ice-cream vans had once been used to procure prostitutes—Amanda had to reassure the locals that all she was selling was ice cream!

She performed on the roof-top stage, raising decorative "balustrades" and setting up the lighting. Amanda had lined up about a dozen gigs along the way, but also had pop-up concerts where it felt right. Altogether she did about sixty shows across the USA on this amazing trip. Her best shows were in Texas, where at one festival the locusts were so loud that she played along with the "crescendo" in the trees. They had to interrupt their journey as Amanda's closest friend was very ill and she wanted to go back to say her goodbyes. Maybe Amanda and Amelia will have another roadtrip adventure, but in the meantime she still sells ice cream and performs at events.

Cris lives in the city of Portland, Oregon. The house she shares with her husband and family has a secluded yard surrounded by mature trees and shrubs—the perfect setting for her natural cob house.

Cris's background is as an artist and sculptor and the idea of helping to construct the cob house and sculpting a beautiful, artistic building really appealed to her. The decision to have a natural build came about some years ago when Cris found her electromagnetic field was interrupting electricity around her. She became interested in healing when it was suggested that she could use this power to good effect. She also felt that an earth building would help ground her and be a place where she could work positively with her healing energy.

In 2003 Cris started building her cob house with Sukita, an expert natural builder who helped design the house. Sukita specializes in the use of natural plasters and floors for any kind of building, but this was her first cob build. The small house took them a few summers to construct, from laying the foundations, building the walls, and putting on the roof. In 2007 they had a party to celebrate its completion.

The foundations were made from a sculpted metal cage filled with rocks, which were then stuccoed on the outside. The cob house was always intended to be a kidney-bean shape to give a generous porch area covered by the circular roof and held up with beautiful "barley twist" columns designed by Cris.

opposite The internal kidney bean-shaped floorplan creates a generous porch, with pillars hand-sculpted by Cris supporting the circular shingle-tiled roof.

right The cob house was built on rock foundations, while the cob walls include clay mostly sourced from the land.

"I come here more now. It balances me and it's a great place to meditate ... and find *peace* and *quiet*."

Much of the mud came from Cris's own land, and the pond in her yard was created where the clay had been dug out. The cob walls are a mixture of this clay, sand, straw, and water, mixed together and built up by hand. The plastering inside and out is a more refined mix known as "aliz" and is painted on for a smoother effect. Mica and white clay were added to the clay wash to seal and beautify the surface, bringing a sparkle and translucence to the walls. Cris loves the fact that the whole house has been sculpted and touched by human hands, adding to the energy of the building.

As with many slow builds, it became organic both in the building and the design. Round windows became sculpted and recessed arched windows; a wood burner was a later addition and, with the under-floor heating and shredded blue-jean insulation, the room is cozy. When the wall across the room detracted from the flow of space and interrupted the good feng shui of the building, they took it down—with another builder and friends, they began sawing, rocking, and pushing until, like discovering an Ancient Egyptian tomb, they broke through to discover a whole new room!

The gems of blue glass in the walls came from blue bottles. Sukita explains, "We drank a lot of lemonade that year!" Cris intended to use 33 bottles as 33 is a "master number," but some of the bottles will never be seen again as she felt "they were a bit tarty!" and so plastered over a number of them.

The cupola, designed by a female friend and now known as the "cute-ola," was created to sit on top of the shingle roof and introduce more natural light into the building. The cedar shingles were a lucky find at a salvage yard and there were enough to allow for some trimming to cover the whole building. Jutting out from under the shingles are beautiful rafter tails, their design based on Cris's memories of travels to Bali, Nepal, Greece, and beyond.

The ceiling treatment is decorative, that is to say that none of the beams on the inside are structural. Rather, they are an evocation of bamboo roofs seen by Cris and her husband on their honeymoon in Thailand. The walls bring to mind memories of a visit to the ancient Greek city of Knossos, while the windows are inspired by traditional English leaded windows. The arched door reminds Cris of a Dutch door from her childhood. The lamps are Moroccan in style and simple enough not to detract from the rest of the room. It's an eclectic mix of memories, with a touch of Hobbit thrown in, which really works.

Cris and her husband have opened three coffee shops in Portland and these took up a lot of energy during the build, but now Cris is finding time to build up her own healing practice in the cob house. She and her husband have taken to sleeping there sometimes and they let friends stay. They always sleep incredibly well in this healing and safe place. Cris says, "I use it more now. It balances me and it's a great place to meditate, and—with a house full of teenagers and their friends—to get some peace and quiet."

above The cupola was a later inspired addition, which lets more light into the house. Built by a woman friend, it came to be called the "cute-ola!"

opposite above The arched windows feature blue lemonade bottles– plenty of lemonade was drunk by thirsty workers during the construction. They create beautiful accents to the recessed carved window surrounds.

opposite below The old wood burner was a lucky find. It was spotted on a lawn, being offered for free, and so it found a new home.

Emily lives in her parents' garden in Gloucestershire, England, in one of two sheds that face each other across a paved area furnished with picnic benches. When she was sixteen years old, her brother moved into the first shed and Emily had a severe case of shed envy. At that time, the second shed belonged to her father, who had it built for his basket making. It took a great deal of persuasion for him to allow Emily to take it over and have her own place, albeit just a few steps from the house.

When he agreed, she took possession of an uninsulated shed that expanded and contracted according to the weather, the temperature, and the moisture. Her parents worried at first, unable to see how it could become a viable home.

Emily began to make it her own. She spent her first week cleaning, moving her Dad's willow out and dismantling everything. "It was horrible!" she exclaims. She wanted a wooden floor, so took up the musty old carpets and discovered a dark brown creosote floor. She borrowed a sander and spent five and a half hours taking it back to the natural wood. A finishing coat of floor protection and it was done. She wanted a distressed floor and she says, "I got a distressed Dad!"

right In her parents' steep hillside garden, steps lead up to Emily's reclaimed shed.

opposite With the doors open in good weather, Emily uses the patio and the tables and chairs as an outside room. When the weather is less accommodating, she can close the doors and be very cozy in her shed.

Emily had previously been a painter-decorator in Scotland, working with people with learning disabilities and helping on a biodynamic farm. There she lived in a caravan, so was used to the practicalities of living in a small space. Emily talks of the conflict between a love of color and space, clutter and coziness.

She insulated, then painted the walls white using eco-paints. Although not normally a lover of white walls, she needed the light and the simple backdrop for her precious paintings and objects, such as her great grandfather's violin. He was a sea captain from Leith, Scotland and made the violin in his spare time. Emily thinks it could date back to the late nineteenth century. Her paintings include her own stormy sea and paintings from her grandparents, which mean a lot to Emily. There is a "detail from the Sistine Chapel" behind the TV and a tapestry rug, which may be Peruvian, hangs above her bed.

Emily made her bed out of pallets, which she assumed would be easy, but as all the pallets were different sizes it took hours to solve the puzzle of how best to fit them together! Hops, originally planted by her mother to help Emily sleep as a child, tumble across the shed exterior and sometimes creep through the window. There is a wonderful mixture of the past and present and Emily is very happy with her live-in shed. "It's my little bubble," she explains. In the summer she throws the doors open and the patio becomes her dining room.

For the last year or so this peaceful haven has been her home, and its handy location means Emily can walk into the nearby town of Stroud, where she works. Despite living so close to her parents' house, she says she doesn't spend much time there. She is in the happy position of being both with her parents yet separate from them.

There is still shed desire in the family. The other shed could become a studio for her leatherwork or somewhere for her mother to take up drawing again ...

above The white walls act as a backdrop for Emily's precious paintings and objects.

inset A pretty dressing table has been created in a corner.

overleaf Emily turned her father's shed into a home.

"It took five and a half hours to get the old creosote off the floor. I wanted a distressed floor and got a distressed Dad!"

Christine has been a herbalist for eighteen years and moved to her house in a pretty village in Norfolk soon after qualifying. She and her partner, Mark, also have a working smallholding just outside the village where they keep chickens, geese, and a few cows, which they rear organically. It is a place of fields and woods, both wild and farmed. There are polytunnels, where Christine brings on her herb seedlings before they are brought back to the herb garden at the house, a number of sheds, and a beautiful timber-clad agricultural building.

The Retreat is a chalet-style building on the smallholding, nestled among trees which were beautifully sun-dappled on the day we visited. Walking through a gap in a wild hedge we came upon this wooden cabin in an idyllic setting of trees and wilderness. Adding to the charm of the place, the cockerel and hens made an entrance from around the back of the cabin. To the side is a stack of logs, ready for the wood burner which keeps the chalet warm in the winter.

This place has been a retreat for friends and family in need at difficult times, and for Christine when she requires peace and a bit of time to herself. It has also provided accommodation for people taking part in the WWOOFA scheme (Willing Workers on Organic Farms).

The chalet is small and doesn't feature an indoor bathroom. As Christine showed us around, she led us through another break in a hedge close to the barn, where we found one of the polytunnels. There, inside the tunnel, sits a clawfoot bath on a floor laid with red bricks and with a shower fixed to a timber upright! And in a wild corner of the land there is a compost toilet. So, one way or another, all amenities are here for anyone wishing to have a few days of seclusion.

opposite The solar panels and a plentiful supply of wood for the wood burner ensure this is a cozy retreat.

right The cabin has all mod cons including a roll-top bath in a nearby polytunnel, surrounded by grapevines.

162 hidden huts and hideaways

"This is my cabin for quiet and solitude among the trees."

"At the bottom of the garden, behind all the trees, I have my own rhythm."

above The materials and personal objects that surround Filipa feed her creative process.

opposite Filipa planted the many trees she loves, creating a small woodland setting for her creative shed in the city.

Filipa has a two-story shed at the bottom of her garden in Cambridge. As a New Yorker, Cambridge really suits her. Apart from work opportunities, it is the diverse population and creative culture that attracted her and Gareth to this English city. When they moved into this house, they needed more room and so Gareth began the build. However, Filipa loves trees and planted "too many" so the shed has gradually disappeared behind a Mongolian birch, a Californian lilac, two hazelnut trees, an early flowering honeysuckle *Fragrantissima*, a pear tree, and a beautiful blue and red *buddleia davidii*.

A path through the semi-wild garden leads to this unusual building. Gareth built the shed out of recycled materials. The interior cladding is probably early Tudor, from the thirteenth century. His father, Selwyn, who is mentioned on pages 68 and 202, had rescued them from an old building. They are ancient oak, felled at a time when there were plenty of oak forests in the UK. The patina, wear, and age make them very uneven and beautiful.

The large windows were found discarded in a dumpster and carried across Cambridge—with some difficulty, as not only are they double glazed but also bulletproof! Gareth used whatever came to hand, including part of an obsolete piano which happened to fit the side of a window as an upright support. The roof is tiled with cedar shingles and the walls are faced with a soft blue-gray tongue and groove. There is a large loft for storage of all the things the family might need at some point in the future. The furniture is found rather than bought.

above As part of a costume for a *butoh* performance at a summer festival, Filipa decorated shoes with crow's feathers.

opposite and inset An old sofa and a wood burner create a comfortable corner to relax in. Floors, walls, shelves, and windowsills are all built from reclaimed wood.

When the three children were young, they held sleepovers and parties here. And when the house was being renovated, the whole family lived in the shed for a winter. The children had a mattress each and a trunk to keep their stuff in. A shed next door housed a bathroom but everything else, including cooking and eating, happened at the bottom of the garden. Filipa recalls, "It felt like living on a strange boat." The green decorative wood burner helped it feel very cozy that winter. Filipa uses the shed all year around, "although January can be quite damp."

Eventually, as the children grew up, Filipa was able to reclaim the shed and she now uses it to store art materials and anything else she needs or loves which doesn't fit into their house. The family wanted to negotiate the space, but she stood her ground. It is her space, although sometimes the children are let in. She can be found working in the shed far into the night, until two or three in the morning when it is very quiet.

Filipa is an artist and dancer, working with people with dementia and with patients in the local hospital. She works across communities with young and old and loves it. The shed is where she is able to gather her ideas. She can leave whatever she is working on on the table, close the door, and return to pick up the threads the next day. Filipa enjoys the pottering process. "I think, create, devise, write, and play my records. I like that it's not far away but I can move to a different frame of mind within a few yards."

There are huge rolls of paper and shelves of books, fabrics, and all sorts of meaningful objects. On the table are gloves and shoes decorated with feathers. Filipa explains, "They are crow's feet and hands for a *butoh* (a slow Japanese dance form) performance I was part of at the Latitude Festival." This is an organized space and Filipa likes boxes, especially old hatboxes. She can see everything and she does know where everything is. There are drapes of old and new cobwebs. "I like the spiders and their webs ... they are quiet!"

Filipa says that the shed helps with her sanity when the house is so busy with family life. At the bottom of the garden behind all the trees, she says, "I have my own rhythm."

"I use the shed all year round, except January when it can be damp."

"I have realized the **vision** within me and building a house was **profound**. I'm showing up. This is Harriet unplugged."

Harriet has a "proper" house in Portland, Oregon, but chooses to live in her backyard Moon Cottage, surrounded by an abundant fruit and vegetable garden. It is slightly wild, but Harriet loves the anarchy of one crop taking over another. Other people now live in the main house, contributing to the growing and preservation of crops. However, the house is still part of her everyday life as she doesn't have a bathroom or kitchen in the cottage.

She built her cottage on the site of a pear tree, with the support of the Village Building Convergence. Their website explains the aims of this collective: "We come together at sites around the city to create natural building, permaculture, and public art projects. These include benches, gardens, street paintings, tile mosaics, and more. Neighbors have been collaboratively designing these projects, creating community with each other in the process. People come from near and far to learn skills and help bring these designs to life, while celebrating creativity and diversity." Harriet adds, "It is a way of taking back the city for community projects."

The cottage is built from Larson framing with a rammed clay and straw filling. The first layer is shuttered, then rammed with the mixture. When that layer is dry, another layer can go on, continuing in this way until the walls reach the desired height. They are then plastered with a clay slip. The internal walls are also clay slip rendered in a soft orange with the wonderful texture of hand plastering.

The stairs to the sleeping loft are made from sustainably grown timber and the beams were sourced at a rebuilding center. Behind the staircase is a sculpted and recessed altar to the pear tree that once grew on this piece of land. The writing in the pear alcove is a Sanskrit saying, speaking of the beauty of the now.

There is also a table altar and Harriet explains the importance of the items displayed there: "The little statue on the left is Shiva dancing. His many arms represent the four Vedas, which are each huge bodies of religious text that make up the Hindi faith. This particular image of Shiva is one of the more popular. Here, Shiva, as male energy, dances only the Tandava while his consort, Parvati, dances the Lasya in

response. But I'll go with the dance (as some suggest) as representing their unified energies symbolizing the five principal manifestations of eternal energy." On the table are other objects she loves. The image in the little watercolor is of Harriet's father and is a copy of a painting her brother commissioned, taken from a photo of her father as a young man. Harriet explains, "My father was a holocaust survivor and was very dear to me in the many lessons he taught me, most significant of which was 'Never give up because the moment you do, you are finished.' He also told me that if you walk into the woods with your troubles, you will walk out without them. He became a benchmark of how much a person can endure in life and yet manage to believe in the future. That is the most remarkable aspect of human nature—its resilience."

The image in the center is Ganesh. "Synchronistically, my son refers to himself as 'Elephant Smiley' in much of his creative work (such as paintings and music) and I doubt he knew the Ganesh image at that time." On the right is an incense burner. The table offers Harriet "a sense of the sacred, the mysterious, the things in life that cannot be seen or known simply through the rational mind alone. And since my mind is rarely rational, that helps."

During the build Harriet produced numerous meals for the many volunteers on site, and the bulk of the building materials were donated or found in salvage yards. Sustainability is the core word for her future plans, including rainwater collection and a compost loo. Volunteers came to learn traditional skills while helping to build her cottage, becoming part of an urban farm family. They learnt to move and farm with the seasons.

The harvest from Harriet's own garden is turned into jams, preserves, and pickles, and this abundance and preservation is all part of her ideology. She believes in and supports other urban farmers, with an emphasis on what she calls "farmers' wives" skills. She adds that this phrase is not intended to be gender specific, but says that farmers tend to know how

to plant and reap, but people also need to learn the skills of preservation of food for the leaner months.

Harriet says that, as an older woman, she has connected to her creative side as she discovers "new spaces." One day she would like to take "baby steps out of Portland" and is "becoming the person I want to date!"

Harriet has found that "I have everything in me. I have my gardens." She has built a garden kitchen and classroom in her garden where she can process her food and teach others. The classroom was constructed using the old garage and behind that is the kitchen, an open-air room with industrial cooking and preserving equipment. Here people can swap fruit and vegetables when they have a glut. It is an excellent way to live in a city.

Harriet loves the fact that the cottage has no internet connection, allowing her to read, write, sleep, or look up and watch the moon rise overhead. With the direction and passion in her life, Harriet says, "I had been up against avoidance until I realized the vision in me. Building a house was profound." She adds, "I'm showing up ... this is Harriet unplugged!"

above Harriet teaches gender-free "farmers' wives" skills, including the preservation of vegetables and fruit, from her garden kitchen and classroom.

Helena lives in a remote part of Suffolk, which suits her and her lifestyle. She found this old Methodist chapel about fifteen years ago. It was in a ramshackle state, but she bought it for the view and employed a builder to shape it to her specifications.

The Chapel sits in "The Pit," located down a rough track which leads away from a small village. There are no major roads nearby and, apart from some day-to-day sounds from her two neighbors, all is silence and in that silence she is able to witness and hear the birds and animals that live around her. It really is all about the view.

"I love the silence and couldn't imagine finding anywhere else so quiet." Helena doesn't have a car or a television. Her philosophy is that we all could lead a much simpler life. She thinks she is, perhaps, not made for the modern world.

It is the "Unmanaged Meadow" that drew her to this site. It gently slopes down to an old agricultural ditch, beyond which cattle graze the meadows. Further on are the woods, through which you can walk to the North Sea.

Late May is the prime time for the meadow. The plants that grow here have wonderful names, including speedwell, knapweed, trefoil, meadowsweet, yellow pea, and the pignut flower—roots of this plant have been eaten over the centuries, cooked or raw (it has a taste rather like a chestnut). Helena is very protective of this area, as she would hate anyone to dig up the southern marsh orchids that nestle in the long grass. A local cowman gathers the hay once a year, once the seeds have been shed.

The double doors of the painting-filled and music-rich converted chapel open out on to a paved area where many, many pots stand, filled with rich colored flowers. These are the only sign of cultivation, although far off behind the shed is a vegetable garden.

above The plain shed sits on the edge of a paved garden, which has a wonderful view of meadows and fields.

"I love the **silence** and couldn't imagine
finding anywhere else **so quiet**."

hidden huts and hideaways 177

When Helena talks about her shed becoming a retreat in the near future, she is philosophical about when that might happen as she is waiting for the "artist builder" to become available. She enjoyed another shed he built for a friend and now she awaits her turn, but he is "painfully slow to come."

She has cleared the shed of most of the clutter that had accumulated over the years. For now, it is a promise and a store. The promise is held in the shabby chairs, which are gathered around a wicker table and face toward the old limewashed wall where, one day, a new large window will face out on to her beloved view. There will be French doors to the patio and these will bring plenty of light to a space where Helena imagines sitting, being, and maybe, one day, taking up writing again as she was encouraged to do when she was younger. With the light will come warmth as she will insulate it well. "It'll be warmer than the house in the winter."

She could play her violin in the new shed, but the chapel has a fantastic acoustic so that's where the music will stay. She wants it to be a simple and uncomplicated space and, to that end, she is keeping the back of the shed as a store for the stuff of life. She says, "I must resist the tendency to fill it up."

For now, she has a chair in the old greenhouse, where she sits and reads on days in the spring and fall when it is not quite warm enough to be outside. Her whole life, she says, is a retreat.

Helena believes that common land should remain intact to conserve the land for nature and for all of our futures. She is a custodian of the meadow and resists the impulse of others to claim parts of it for their own land. Working with the Suffolk Wildlife Trust, she manages it in a hands-off and benign fashion, watching the seasons and plants change. The wonderful meadow plants attract birds and butterflies, such as the comma butterfly. Kingfishers have been seen along the ditch, and a barn owl flies overhead and feels like a friend.

"Saving this bit of unimproved hay meadow makes my life worthwhile. The hay is gathered once a year by a local cowman once the seeds have been shed."

"The courtyard catches the sun all day ...
and I love to have friends round for coffee
or a glass of wine there."

In the small Suffolk town of Eye there is a very pretty street consisting of a few shops and two rows of old houses, many of which are listed as having historical interest. The worlds behind these houses are hidden from general view, and many are only accessible through gated archways. **Wendy** loves living in this location, where she can emerge through the archway from her little garden and find everything she needs in the town. She was brought up on a farm with horses and so this little oasis of nature is very important to her.

In Wendy's garden, an open archway leads first to a courtyard and then to a tiny garden. Her bespoke shed came with her from her old house when she moved here four years ago and, amazingly, fitted into this new space with less than an inch to spare. The "wonderful" builder who lived next door was the hero of the hour!

Wendy painted the shed a gentle gray-green to act as a soft background to the foliage. Mirrors hanging on trellises create a sense of space and the orientation of the garden means that there is sun for most of the day. Her favorite time of day is morning, when the courtyard is flooded with light. This is the area where Wendy tends to many pots of plants and flowers, including clematis, lupins, poppies, geraniums, aquilegia, and later there will be roses.

Wendy's house is also tiny and the shed has become her "isle of peace"—a place where she can take her coffee or, maybe later, a glass of wine and look back to the trellised pink walls of the house and decide what to move to where and which plants need her attention. The shed's double doors might be closed for privacy or flung open on fine days.

Inside the shed is a table, with a storage trunk underneath. Shelves hold her collection of vases, with the right one always to hand for her flowers of choice. A decorative mirror reflects the light and brings the garden in.

"It's a place of great pleasure and gives me tremendous joy!"

above The shed is full
of books, vases, and
gardening equipment,
yet still has room for
Wendy's chair and a table
for the current novel and
a cup of coffee.

opposite This pretty
little courtyard is packed
with plants and flowers,
lovingly attended to and
moved to their best
advantage according to
the seasons.

There are folding chairs, gardening equipment, magazines, gardening books, and, lying on the table by her chair, a novel for that moment when the doors are wide open, the sun is shining, her coffee or wine are at hand, and she is taken into another world.

Wendy says that people laugh at her collections of vases, pots, plants, and the many objects in the house. She has a huge abundance in every nook and cranny. She explains she has been a collector all her life, and enjoys moving things about and rearranging her treasured possessions. When she feels anxious, she can go to her place of refuge and think, "rather like thinking about things as you do in the bath." Moving things, thinking, making lists—all these lead to a sense of peace.

Wendy is sociable and really enjoys entertaining. She has been known to host a dinner party for eight in this outside space but she says of her guests, "They all have to go to the loo first, as once seated they will stay put until the end!" Candles light up the space for the diners, but although a candlelit night is romantic, she is thinking about putting in electricity so that she can heat the shed on cold days and get more use out of her refuge.

Every year the town hosts an Open Gardens weekend, where the hidden gardens can be explored, from the grand to the tiny. In the preceding year Wendy had about 500 people visiting the shed and her abundant little courtyard of plants. To add to the appeal for visitors, Wendy has put up bunting, which gives the shed a beach-hut feel. She says, "It is a place of great pleasure and gives me tremendous joy!"

Sue found this property just by chance when she saw it featured in a local magazine. She and **Janet** went to see it and fell in love with it. First there was the birdsong, then they walked around the corner and knew, "This is it!"

This secret garden, near a beach in Suffolk, is entirely hidden by the dunes. On one side is the North Sea, on the other side are the salt marshes. The gate says "Private" and gives no hint of the extent or wonder of this wilderness, the sheds, and the wagon.

There were others who were interested in buying the plot and the price was high. However, these potential buyers wanted it as a development investment and hoped to build on it. This was never going to be, not least because of occasional flooding from the sea, so the seller had to readjust his expectations and sell at a price Sue and Janet could afford. And so they got their "Secret Field," so tucked away that locals didn't even know that it was there. When invited in, they are invariably "gobsmacked!"

It is the wilderness that enchants them. They have an owl box—when we visited, a Little Owl and her chicks were in residence, with the male flying in regularly with food for the brood. Janet has set up cameras in the owl box, which are rigged so that she can play back the previous night's activity on the computer in the wagon. Her cameras can also be found in another secluded spot where badgers and their cubs come to feed and play. Just a little light dusting is needed to keep the lenses clear of cobwebs, to avoid a close-up spider marring the shots. Sue and Janet built their own hide so that they can watch the badgers. There is also a straw-bale playground, which the

right The summerhouse is as light as can be with huge windows on three sides. The white paint and pale colors further add to this feeling of openness and space.

below The hidden field is tucked behind a wild, wide, and remote beach in Suffolk.

opposite below The summerhouse was already on the field when Sue discovered this magical world of meadows and hedges

Janet's traveler's wagon was also already in situ when they bought the field. It has a deep indigo blue and dark green exterior and the interior walls are paneled with wood, some of which is textured where white paint has been scraped back. They had to renovate the wagon and make sure it was waterproof and insulated, but ensured that none of its original charm was lost during renovation. At one end is Janet's workbench where she uses her laptop to record and film the wildlife. There are wildlife photos all over the walls around the bench which attest to her fascination, and, on a nearby chest, an experiment in capturing badgers' footprints on paper.

Sue and Janet say they will never leave the field, preferring to let it go wild when they can no longer take care of it. Sue says, "If there was not another life, I would spend all my time here." As it is, they visit everyday, whatever the weather, to tend to the veggie patch, for Janet to see who visited the night before, or simply just to hang out. They have come to know the local community, who are delighted they are there. The gate, though, is shut and the locals won't just pop in. They respect the privacy these two women have created. After all, it was the field and the community that led them to find a house in a nearby village.

above left The traveler's wagon was the first hut Sue and Janet saw when they first visited the field.

above Janet watches and records sightings of the wildlife that visits their land.

"If there was not another life,
I would spend all my time here."

In Norfolk, in the city of Norwich, there is a hidden garden and a small retreat where **Sally** spends her days. The house is full of lodgers, which she loves, but that means there is very little space she can call her own. This pale blue summerhouse, which she uses for her business, is at the end of a stepping-stone path curving across the grass—her and the cat's journey to and from work every day. Sally is a copy editor and proofreader, working mostly with academic writing. To contrast with that work, she is also an EFT (Emotional Freedom Technique) practitioner and uses this healing technique with her clients.

above Sally sits at her desk working and looking out over her beautiful mature garden, while Seed the cat curls up and sleeps nearby.

opposite The gently curving path crosses the lawn leading to the summerhouse, which is framed by trees separating Sally from the city all around her.

When Sally moved here nearly a quarter of a century ago, the garden contained three apple trees that weren't in the best of health. Twenty four years later, Sally has established a mature garden which gives her the privacy she desires. On one side of her English garden, there is a very high hedge and, at the end of the garden, an archway that gives the illusion of further adventures but, in reality, leads through the remains of an ancient hedgerow to the roads and houses beyond.

Sally's late mother surprised her by leaving her enough money to buy this traditional garden summerhouse. She is to be found here nearly every day, with Seed, her Somali cat, for company. Seed follows her everywhere and is "utterly my friend." To make it suitable for year-round use, the shed has been insulated and relined with unpainted wooden tongue-and-groove boards. It is furnished with two gray armchairs for visitors and clients, and her working chair, desk, and computer.

Displayed on the walls are two pieces of writing that are meaningful to Sally. One says, "We would like you to reach the place where you're not willing to listen to people criticize one another ... where you take no satisfaction from someone being wrong" from an Abraham-Hicks publication. This quotation is an inspiration to Sally. A philosophy of positive thinking guides her life. "I concentrate on beauty over the tough issues of life."

The summerhouse is a place where she "likes to be free and laugh" in what she describes as her and Seed's haven. Sally can work here all day and absolutely loves it. She explains, "Not in a paranoid way, but it's a hideaway from the student lodgers in the house. It is totally my space."

The view of the beautiful garden feeds the eyes—peonies, aquilegias, azaleas, pink weigela, foxgloves, and white viburnum fill the borders. There are both tamed and wild plants changing throughout the year, and the curved path gives the view a parabolic shape, leading the eye through this very private vista. It is a garden that calls to her to leap out of her chair to do a bit of this and that. The visiting wildlife of the city also makes Sally happy. "One evening there was a baby fox out there, and I've even seen a muntjac deer. There are hedgehogs, frogs and newts, and many birds. Spotting a buzzard or a goldcrest lifts the heart."

Sherry has a farm in Happy Valley near Portland, Oregon, with her husband Scott. It has been in her family for generations, all the way back to the years of the Oregon Trail. Pendarvis Farm was one of the first farms settled in the mid-nineteenth century.

Behind a barn on the property is an old bus, nestling into the hillside. This is where Sherry retreats and sleeps during the annual Pickathon Indie Roots Festival, which she hosts on her land. This huge music festival was due to start the day after our visit. Stages set up in barns, sky sculptures, and a recording studio up in the woods were ready to go.

The bus has enjoyed previous lives—a school bus, a bus for the Green Tortoise bus tour company, and a "hippy bus" traveling up and down the west coast. It even went to The Burning Man Festival in Nevada several times. Visiting friends arrived at the farm with the bus and parked it. It got stuck in the mud, then it wouldn't start, and that was it. Sherry says they were "aghast" at first, but being green helped. The friends hadn't got anywhere to store it, so Sherry bought it. She likes to think of the bus as a "virtual tour bus"—it doesn't travel, but Sherry likes to imagine it could. It also doubles as a meeting room when Sherry wants some privacy away from the chaos of the festival. Her bed is at the far end of the bus with bookshelves and a door that can be shut to close off the area. Then she can open the back doors of the bus and enjoy the magnificent view of Mount Hood to the north.

Sherry enjoys the colored cloths she drapes over the seats and at the windows. "They wouldn't go in our more subdued house." This and the eccentricities of the bus, such as the huge deer head on the engine cover and the fluffy steering wheel taking them nowhere, are expressions of complete freedom to do anything just for the fun of it.

Sherry likes the change of skyscape each year as the sky sculptures are different for each festival. Climbing on top of the bus allows great views, and during the festival she might invite a rock star or friend up there.

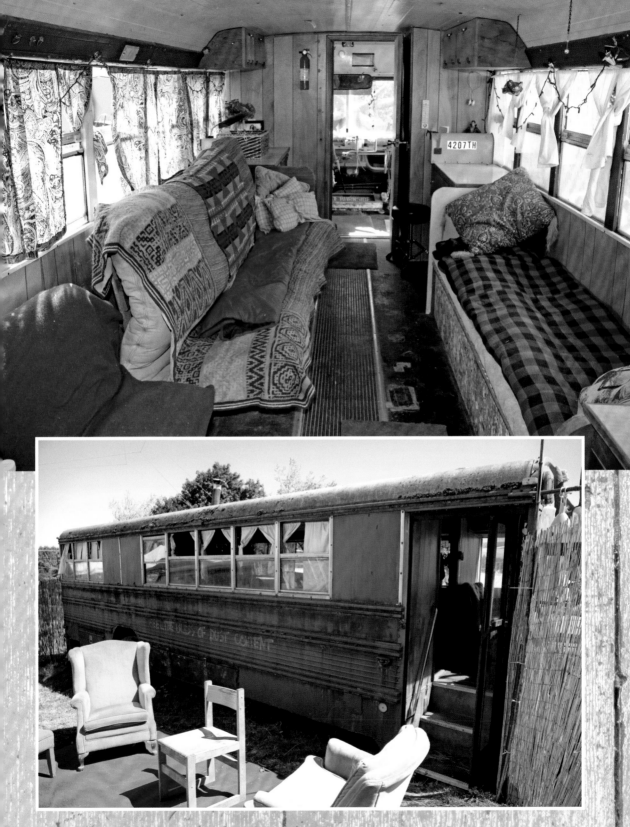

above A walk through the woods takes you to the Red Dog recording studio, hidden away from festival activity.

right The Red Dog is where musicians hang out. There are armchairs and sofas for comfort and a large carpet defines the outside room.

opposite A ghostly hare plays a piano under sky sculptures.

overleaf Empty frames hang on invisible walls.

The bus means that Sherry is close enough to the action to be available if necessary, but has privacy. The interior is undesigned and comfortable and a woodstove keeps it warm in colder weather (only November and December are too cold for overnight stays in the bus). A nearby barn provides a bathroom and shower, as the main house is too far away if Sherry and her husband just want to fall into bed after hanging out or partying. Lighting is powered from solar panels on the barn and Sherry says, "I love to read up here. We work hard to get the festival going and when it starts, you want to be done."

Sherry feels the bus has a sense of humor, and is whimsical and light-hearted. She notes, "It is hard to get into an argument in this wacky and funny bus."

The bus is just for Sherry and Scott to sleep in, but there is space elsewhere on the farm for many guests—in the house, in a barn, and in Red Dog. Red Dog is an old pump house that was once used to provide water for the cattle, but today it acts as a recording studio during the festival and as a retreat at other times. It is hidden along a path, through some woods, and up a hill. During the festival it comes to life with lights, recording equipment, outdoor staging, and an outside sitting room fully equipped with sofas, armchairs, a coffee table, and even a window hanging in the trees. Lampshades are scattered here and there and, behind the musicians' area, picture frames and paintings hang in the trees on invisible walls. It is a wonderful and surreal environment.

Sherry likes the acoustics and jam parties where she plays stringed instruments and keyboards—"I play a lot of things." The lighting and power for Red Dog, when the festival is on, is provided by a generator, but at other times it is off-grid and lamps and candles light the hut at night,

Sherry knows the land here like the back of her hand and says she could find Red Dog in the dark. "If I want to avoid people, this is another place I can come," she says. "It'll be somewhere to go when the zombie war starts!"

Back in 1969 **Lorraine** and her husband, Selwyn, bought a near-derelict row of cottages set back from heathland in the Waveney Valley in Suffolk. Selwyn renovated many buildings in his time and these were some of them.

There was originally only an old pigsty and some beehives on the land. Soon Selwyn found the cattle truck in a railway stock sale, and then bought the traveler's wagon in a local auction. This wagon may well have been a roadmender's sleeping wagon. Lorraine explains that similar wagons ended up in California, and were often turned into cafés.

She sometimes stayed in the old wagon in order to get away from the chaos of the building work at the cottages, finding refuge among the willows and the two beloved oak trees nearby. One winter she lived there for a while and read *Remembrance of Things Past*—Marcel Proust's long French novel in seven parts—by candlelight.

By the time the cottages were finally renovated and sold, Lorraine had made an emotional attachment to the secluded wild spot and decided to keep this piece of land. It's not a huge plot, but it is entirely hidden, even from people walking their dogs on the nearby heath.

right and inset The old wagon was one of Selwyn's many finds at a farm sale and it may have been a cattle truck in the past. Nowadays it is an indoor room where Lorraine can write or take refuge if the weather is too bad to sit outside. Family love to be here and sit around the fire pit at night.

"My family and Selwyn's friends come here to remember him ... there are no gates, but people respect this place. I will cling to it with what little passion I have left."

She keeps it a secret, shared with only a few chosen guests or friends of her husband who want to visit and remember him. To find it, if you were allowed, you go along a potholed bumpy track before reaching the nettled path leading to Lorraine's land. There is a mown path through the nettles and then a climb over a low bar before the green oasis opens up before you. There are no signs to keep out and no gate, yet the place is respected and no one wanders in. The heathland is designated as a Site of Special Scientific Interest and is therefore protected as wild land in perpetuity. Lorraine is re-learning birdsong so that she can identify the birdlife.

For Lorraine the meaning of this special place centers around memory, family, and time and space for herself. In this secluded spot, she can get away from the world. It is a place for reflection and meditation. She now lives in the nearby town and has no garden, so this is where she comes to be in nature, to think, and to write. There is a stone for Selwyn, who is buried on the land. The extended family comes together here. The generations share picnics and memories, laugh and play in this special oasis. Lorraine would never let the land go and may well choose to end up there next to Selwyn. She says she loves it "with the little passion I have left!" Her enthusiasm and joy for the place shine.

Family will mow from time to time, cut back fallen and invasive willow, and tidy up the edges, but it is wild and meant to be that way. There are nettles and cow parsley everywhere. Where willows have fallen in high winds, there are gaps to be filled with new trees. It's used all year around, but in the winter months Lorraine visits less often since the cattle truck has no heating and no electricity, only a small solar panel which needs fixing, so evenings are lit by candles. When the family meet at night, they gather around the fire pit and the flames create a warm and wonderful center of dancing firelight.

With its rust-red exterior and large, studded, double wooden doors, the cattle truck nestles against the shrubbery. It is furnished with items brought ad hoc by family and visitors, much of which ends up outside in good weather, so there is a charm from the mismatch of finds. "A horrible pink armchair turned up" and is considered "revolting," but there it sits among other chairs. The "horrible" chair was once the source of inspiration for a film made by and with grandchildren. The wooden floor has an old pink carpet—another find. There is a tin-topped table where Lorraine can write, and a gas tabletop cooker works for meals, mulled wine, and the inevitable cups of tea.

The traveler's wagon has now fallen into disrepair as the cattle truck has become the retreat of choice, but it will be repaired and renovated. In the meantime, the iron framework and sound roof will keep it safe. The roof light will eventually let the light flood back into the wagon and it will be used again.

This is a place of memory, creativity, solitude, and family gatherings, and Lorraine feels safe in this totally private place whenever she chooses to take time out of her busy life for herself.

above The old traveler's wagon has fallen into disrepair and awaits renovation, but meanwhile it has a strong iron structure and a weatherproof roof to protect it from the elements.

Index

Acknowledgments

On this second adventure of meeting women with huts and hideaways, in the USA and UK, I want to thank everyone who has supported the writing of this book including dear friends and family. Most of all a big thank you to all you women, some I know well, and some who we met as complete strangers, who allowed me into their gardens, yards, and waterside huts and homes. I have loved your stories and feel privileged that you allowed us in.

Last but not least I would like to thank all the huts and hideaways owners and builders: Janet Addison, Celeste B, Wendy Black, Susan Bowerman, Michelle Boyle (Michelle's tiny house in Sherwood Oregon designed by Michelle), Lorraine Burr, Cris Chapman (Cob Cottage in Portland Oregon, designed by Cris Chapman, co-designed and built by Sukita Crimmel, Brandon Smyton, Jack Inglis and many other loving hands), Pam Davis McAllister (floating home dedicated to her son, Brandon Allen McAllister, 1976–2012), Canny D, Helena D, Rosa Davis, Harriet Fasenfest (Moon Cottage designed by Wolfgang Kahler and built by volunteers during Village Building Convergence 2013), Filipa, Mary George (beach hut designed by Mary George and built by Simon Neale), Emily Graves (built by her father designed and decorated by Emily), Elly Hargreave, Christine Herbert, Anne Holden (Strawbale buildings designed by Anne Holden and Bob Cowlin and Assington Mill restoration architect Hilary Brightman), Anita Howard (www.lilypadplanet.com built by Walt Quade of Small Home Oregon), Susanna L, Martha Lightfoot (studio designed and built by Steve Birkbeck), Donna N, Fidelis Nyinakasingye, Judith O'Keefe, Karin P, Julia Paul, Sherry Pendarvis (Pendarvis Farm), Julie Reynolds (Airstream Caravan supplied by eurostreamcaravans.co.uk), Polly Robbins ("The Boathouse", designed and constructed by James Robbins and Polly Allen Robbins), Ivy S, Sally S, Lindsey Simon, Marie Smith (Gypsy Caravan restored by Will Windell, The Hideout built by Marie, Mark and Martin Wyard, and Shepherd's Hut built by Jon Everett of "Lovehutlife"), Amanda Stanaway (Ice Cream Ladies owner), Monica Suswin (Cabin on the Hill designed and built by Mark Haughton), Alex Watson (of I Sew Love That Upholstery Studio built by Jon Everett), Janet Watson, Joceline Wickham, Leah Wild (cabin designed by Leah), and Ellie Wyatt.